Volcanic Kitchens

A further collection of recipes, stories and photographs

Gerhard and Henrietta Egger

Foreword

By Jill Nicholas QSM
Journalist and sometime kitchen thrill seeker

When Gerhard and Henrietta (Henri) Egger set out to produce their first *Volcanic Kitchens* colour plated recipe book they hadn't the slightest notion it would be a best seller, let alone the sell-out it was.

That was in 2012 and it came served up with lashings of professional chef/photographer Gerhard's stunning pictures of the people, food and landscape that captures the essence of this unique volcanic and geothermally active region of ours.

Eight years on they have returned to the keepers of local kitchens to provide a second helping of dishes they love to make. Some contributors are seasoned Volcanic Kitchener's who donated samplings of their sought after offerings first time around. Others are making their print debut in its sequel *Volcanic Kitchens, A futher collection of recipes, stories and photographs*.

Whatever their category, virtually all contributors have one thing in common, they're not trained chefs with a string of qualifications in haute cuisine or degrees in scientific gastronomy. Rather, they are enthusiastic home cooks, their domain the typical multi-cultural cooking pot this country's kitchens have become. These are places where the food they create is for family and friends, not commercial gain.

Their offerings are interspersed with dashes of this and that from the Eggers' extensive collection of international dishes.

The 80-plus who have participated in this second Volcanic Kitchens project ascribe to the theory that sharing is one of cookery's great joys. Some recipes are reincarnations of those inherited from the generations that went before or torn from newspapers or magazines, now yellowed by age.

Others have reproduced favourite, more modern dishes, quick to whip up for families on the run, frequently with an inventive twist of their own. Which prompts the rhetorical question is there such as thing as an original recipe or are they simply variations on themes that have stood the test of time and taste buds?

Although much of this book was sourced and complied before the word Covid-19 entered our vocabulary via the deadly global pandemic the virus generated, it had an upside. The resulting seven week lockdown brought a renewed hunger for 'home made' with the kitchen once again the epicentre of our homes. This in turn, has led to food of the kind the Volcanic Kitchens series features becoming more sort after than ever. Long may the pleasure of discovering DIY cookery skills remain.

Like its predecessor that claimed the title of Best Photography Cookbook in New Zealand and was a finalist at the Gourmand World Cookbook Awards, *Volcanic Kitchens, A further collection of recipes, stories and photographs*—has been stylishly produced by an Austrian-Kiwi couple blessed with an acute social conscious that binds them to their community and those who live within it.

In a fine example of community spirit the Eggers are making a number of copies available to a range of local organisations large and small (including the Rotorua Community Hospice) to sell as a fundraiser. All the more reason for us to help make it another best seller from their stable of prize winning, food-related titles.

The talented Eggers have again brought us a beautifully presented work of culinary and pictorial excellence to relish.

We believe food plays an essential role in our community; it brings us together, shapes our memories and empowers us. Regardless of ethnicity, age or gender—people connect over food. Food so often creates the link which binds communities together, and sharing your meal or offering food to others is seen as a welcoming and comforting gesture. It is also a way of sharing your heritage and culture. All the recipes have been submitted by people presently residing here or who had some previous affiliation with Rotorua; they may have lived here in the past.

This new edition of Volcanic Kitchens is about connecting our community through food and photography. Rotorua has a very diverse community—a vibrant Maori culture of which we are proud, and a significant number of residents who identify as Kiwi's but whakapapa back to a variety of nationalities—either through family immigrating to New Zealand in years gone by or because they themselves have chosen to immigrate here.

One just has to visit town during Diwali celebrations or for the Chinese New Year, to see how the community embrace and enjoy what each culture brings. On a summer Thursday evening, visit the Night Market where Nabih Mansur—originally from Palestine, enjoys sharing his culture through his food stall.

A community is not only about people and food, our environs also have a huge impact on the way we live and relate to each other. Gerhard's photographs throughout the book illustrate the scenic beauty of the wider Rotorua/Taupō Volcanic region.

Gerhard and Henrietta Egger
Rotorua

Contents

Rotorua and the Taupō Volcanic Zone

Haere mai ki Rotorua

Rotorua, a city of some 75,000 residents geographically situated in the centre of New Zealand's Taupō Volcanic Zone, is unique in New Zealand. A city with a rich environmental footprint created by the surrounding geothermal activity, an area of beautiful lakes and rivers, forests and native bush.

The Taupō Volcanic Zone has been active for some two million years and is still highly active, as has been witnessed with the 2019 eruption of the eastern volcanic island, Whakaari/White Island. The zone includes the volcanoes of Putauaki/Mt Edgecumbe, Mt Tarawera, and the Tongaririo National Park; Mt Tongariro, Mt Ngāuruhoe and Mt Ruapehu. Mt Ruapheu's last major eruption was in the winter of 1996.

The first settlers to the area came from the Polynesian homeland known as Hawaiki on the Te Arawa waka, captained by Tamatekapua (Tama), eventually settling on the east cost of the North Island in the estuary of the Kaituna River. The first pā was established on the headland and named Maketū. The descendants were great explorers and used the rivers to navigate inland, many settling around the lakes and thermal areas of what is now known as Rotorua. The Māori saying goes "Ko te ihu o te waka kei Maketū, ko te kei o te waka kei Tongariro", the prow of the waka is at Maketū and the stern at Mt Tongariro. Local Māori have for centuries, used the steam and boiling water for cooking and washing. This is still practised today with food being cooked in steam boxes—on the marae this is an easy way of cooking for large numbers of people. Maketū, now a small seaside village is a short drive away and the Kaituna Estuary and Pacific Ocean are popular for the harvesting of kai moana (seafood). The mountains of the Tongaririo National Park which rise prominently from the southern shores of Lake Taupō are popular for the more adventurous; skiing, tramping, mountain biking—and of course fly fishing.

The city of Rotorua sits on the edge of Lake Rotorua; the full name of the lake is Te Rotorua-nui-a-Kahumatamomoe meaning 'Second lake' discovered by Kahumatamomoe, the uncle of the Māori chief Ihenga, the ancestral explorer of the Te Arawa. Lake Rotorua is the 2nd largest lake in the North Island (Lake Taupō being the largest lake in New Zealand) and the largest of the 18 lakes in the area. In the centre of the lake is Mokoia Island, formerly known as Te Motutapu-a-Tinirau. The island is sacred to the people of Te Arawa and is now a wildlife sanctuary for many threatened species including the tīeke (saddleback) and the toutouwai (North Island Robin). For residents however, the island is best known for the love story between a high-ranking Māori chief's daughter, Hinemoa and her love Tūtānekai, a young warrior of lowly birth. Read the love story written by one of their descendants, Paraone Pirika on page 164.

Rotorua has long been a tourism centre (probably the first in New Zealand). The town was already famous in the mid 1800's with international tourists travelling by boat to see the 'eighth wonder of the world'; the Pink and White Terraces on the edge of Lake Rotomahana. The terraces were destroyed in the volcanic activity of the eruption of Mt Tarawera in 1886. Local villages were decimated with many deaths and those that did survive, were displaced. The story of Mt Tarawera is told by Ken Raureti of Ngāti Rangitihi, on page 144.

Today tourists continue to flock to the region and there are many geothermal areas to visit including; Waimangu, Wai-O-Tapu, Hells Gate, Te Puia and Whakarewawera. Kuirau Park in the centre of town provides easily accessible evidence of Rotorua's volcanic history. Here clouds of steam drift across local roads and pathways, mud bubbles behind fenced off structures, pools of water boil and steam escapes the fumaroles. The footbaths fed by the hot mineral waters are where tourists and locals can sit and soak sore feet.

Rotorua is also an adventure playground with a wide variety of outdoor activities. The Redwoods Whakarewarewa Forest hosts the earliest mountain bike park to be built in New Zealand, this now has over 160 kms of trails to suit all ages and abilities. Kayakers and those who love white water rafting enjoy the Kaituna River. Fishermen come from all over the world to catch the 'big one', the lakes, rivers and streams are world renown for the size and quality of trout caught. Whatever you enjoy doing; soaking in a hot pool, walking, running, biking, hiking, swimming, kayaking, fishing, boating, rowing—the list is endless—there is something here for everyone.

Ngā mihi nui

Top right: Whakaari/White Island   Bottom right: Mt Ruapehu   Overleaf: Kuirau Park

Spring

Asparagus Tart

2 sheets puff pastry
2 bunches fresh asparagus
300g fresh tomatoes,
(large meaty varieties are best)
40g feta
olive oil
basil pesto (see page 54)

Preheat oven to 220° C.

Cut pastry sheet into a rectangle approximately 17cm x 32cm and place on a prepared baking tray. Cut two narrow strips of pastry, approximately 3cm wide, brush bottom with a little water and lay on top of each of the long edges of the tart base as a border.

Slice the fresh tomatoes into 1cm thick slices and arrange on top of the tart base. Cut the asparagus tips, long enough to lay across the tart. Brush with olive oil and then sprinkle the crumbled feta over the top.

Place in oven, reduce the heat to 200° C. Bake for 10 - 12 minutes until baked through.

Drizzle with basil pesto to serve.

Cheese Straws

Jill Nicholas

Like so many others I inherited my mother's "go to" recipe collection with a fair few of the gems it contains gleaned from friends or torn out of newspapers and magazines. I'm amused to note Mum began hers in 1936 when she married. 80 plus years on, the ads beside some of the printed offerings are priceless yet most of the contents have stood the test of time—all in imperial measurements of course.

I never knew a time in my mother's life when there wasn't a tin chock full of cheese straws. This recipe from her sacred hoard is written in pencil in what I seem to recall was her mother's handwriting. It's so faded it's virtually impossible to read. Obviously Mum must have committed it to memory, of course she would after making it so often.

3 oz grated cheese
3 oz butter
3 oz flour
yolk of an egg
salt and cayenne to taste
water to mix

Rub butter into flour, add cheese and seasonings.
Beat up yolk with water.
Stir in flour and make stiff paste.
Roll out and cut into narrow strips.
Place on cold tray and bake in a moderate oven until pale brown.

Asparagus Rolls

Joanne Bryant

Asparagus rolls, a kiwi tradition. A platter of these are always found on the table when attending a traditional 'bring a plate' community social occasion.

250g cream cheese
½ tsp onion stock
⅛ tsp garlic salt
⅛ tsp salt
2 tsp Worcestershire Sauce
4 slices bacon, fried to crisp and then chopped finely
sandwich bread
fresh or tinned asparagus
butter for spreading
Parmesan cheese and paprika for garnish

Combine the first 6 ingredients. Flatten the sandwich bread with a rolling pin and cut off the crust. Butter one side of each slice and turn over.

Spread on the cream cheese mixture and place one asparagus spear on each slice. Roll up. Place on baking tray, sprinkle with Parmesan cheese and paprika.

Bake for 15 minutes at 180° C.

Prawn, Mango and Asparagus Salad

Maureen Cresswell

This is another one of those recipes torn out of a newspaper many years ago and enjoyed in spring and over the summer months.

1 clove garlic, peeled and finely chopped
2 spring onions, thinly sliced
2 birds eye chillies, chopped
2 tbsp palm sugar
2 tbsp fish sauce
2 limes zested and juiced
1 mango, peeled and chopped
lightly cooked asparagus sliced on an angle
1 ripe but firm avocado, cubed (optional)
small handful coriander and mint leaves
garlic butter
¼ cup rice flour, seasoned
4 or 5 prawns per person
¼ cup roasted peanuts, chopped

In a bowl mix garlic, onions, chillies, palm sugar, fish sauce, lime juice and zest. Mix together until sugar dissolved.

Add the mango, asparagus and herbs, avocado (if using) and marinate for 30 minutes.

Melt the butter in a frying pan over gentle heat, dip the prawns in the seasoned flour, cook until they have changed colour.

Heap the salad onto a platter, add the cooked prawns and scatter with chopped peanuts before serving.

Green Spaghetti

Nicola Smallwood
Hospice Fundraising & Marketing Manager

This easy and delicious meal is based on a Chelsea Winter recipe and you don't feel like you're eating a bag of spinach!

If using nuts, dry fry them. Pop the butter and olive oil in a frying pan, add onion and garlic and cook on a low heat for 10 minutes until really soft and golden. Chop the spinach and cook in boiling water for a minute. Squeeze out the excess moisture from the spinach (this always burns your hands so I run it under cold water or wait a little bit).

Place everything (bar the spaghetti) in a food processor and blend until it's a chunky paste.

Cook the spaghetti, mix in the sauce and voila! Squeeze some lemon and grate some extra Parmesan on top.

½ cup of pine nuts
(I use any other nuts that are cheaper or sometimes omit them completely)
25g butter
1 tbsp olive oil
1 onion
4 cloves of garlic
400g spinach
1 bunch of basil
(I only use this when basil is in season, otherwise sometimes I've tried other herbs)
¼ cup olive oil
zest of a lemon
1 tbsp lemon juice
¾ cup Parmesan (never scrimp on this)
spaghetti

Asparagus, Barley and Broad Bean Salad

Diana Edwards

Bring pearl barley/orzo and 3½ cups of water to a boil and cook until tender (approximately 20 minutes if quick cooking barley, otherwise will take 40 - 50 minutes), drain.

Cook asparagus until just tender. Cook broad beans in boiling water for 3 - 4 minutes until just tender.

Mix together lemon zest and olive oil for the dressing.

Arrange together the pearl barley/orzo, asparagus, broad beans and pine nuts and lightly toss with the dressing. Season to taste with salt and pepper.

1½ cups pearl barley (can also use orzo)
2 bunches asparagus
¾ cup of broad beans
zest of one lemon
½ cup olive oil
½ cup pine nuts, lightly toasted
salt and ground black pepper

Stuffed Courgettes

If you have a vegetable garden and grow courgettes you will know that if not harvested in time, they grow quickly into giant marrows!

2 tbsp olive oil
1 small onion, finely diced
1 clove garlic, finely chopped
4 small - medium sized courgettes
½ red pepper, diced
2 tbsp sweet chilli sauce
440g can cooked black beans, strained
(you should have around 1½ cups of beans)
2 tsp fresh coriander leaves, chopped
pinch fresh thyme
2 tbsp grated Parmesan

Cut the courgettes in half lengthwise and scoop the flesh out using a small spoon. Finely dice the courgette flesh. Flatten off the bottom of the courgettes so that they sit firm and flat on a baking tray.

Sauté the onion and garlic in olive oil, add diced courgette, red pepper, chilli sauce and beans. Continue cooking until all liquid has evaporated, remove from heat and add thyme and coriander.

Fill the courgette cases with the prepared mixture and then sprinkle with the Parmesan cheese.

Bake in the oven for around 10 minutes until cooked.

Tom Kha with Noodles and Thai Herbs

Theo Vos and Mariëtte Derksen

This is a recipe adapted from Megan May's cookbook *The Unbakery*. We prefer to cook our food rather than eating it raw, so this version was born. It has lovely flavours and that great Thai aroma. An all-round favourite we eat regularly after our sauna.

1 tbsp oil
1 stalk lemongrass
1 medium onion, thinly sliced
1½ tbsp fresh ginger, minced
1 red chilli pepper, minced
4 cloves garlic, minced
2 cm fresh turmeric, finely sliced
1½ cups thinly sliced shiitake mushrooms
1 kaffir lime leaf,
(central stem removed and leaf finely cut)
6 cups vegetable broth, or water with stock cube
½ cup light coconut milk
1 tbsp miso paste
lime peel
1 can tomatoes
2 - 3 tbsp soy sauce
35g zucchini or kelp noodles
1 carrot, julienned
⅓ cup red lentils, well rinsed
sesame oil
fresh coriander leaves
spring onion, chopped
squeeze of lime juice

Cut stalk of lemongrass in half, and then halve again lengthwise, you can tie it up with food-grade twine so that it is easily removed before serving. Heat a large pot over medium heat and once hot, add the oil. Add lemongrass and onion and sauté for 5 minutes, stirring occasionally, the onions should become translucent and soft. Add fresh ginger, chilli peppers, garlic, turmeric, shiitake mushrooms, kaffir lime leaf and sauté for 4 - 5 minutes, stirring occasionally. Add vegetable broth, coconut milk, a few slices of lime peel, tomatoes, soy sauce, miso paste, carrot, lentils, salt (if needed) and stir to combine. Bring back to the boil, then reduce to a simmer, cover and cook for 10 minutes.

Add the noodles and simmer until cooked. Taste and adjust the flavours as needed. Remove lemongrass and lime peel before serving using a large slotted spoon or a fork.

To serve; drizzle with sesame oil and top with coriander leaves, spring onion and a squeeze of lime juice.

Store leftovers covered in the refrigerator for up to 5 days or in the freezer up to 1 month. Reheat on the stove top,

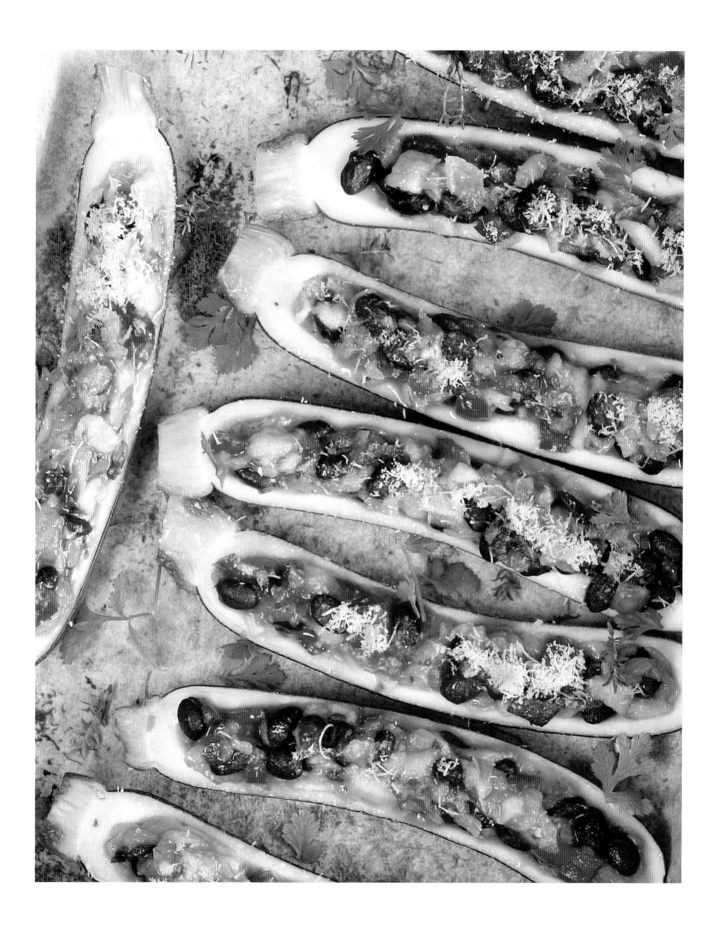

Spring Couscous Salad

This salad uses Israeli couscous, the pearls are larger than Moroccan couscous and have more texture.

Couscous
2 tbsp olive oil
1 clove garlic, finely chopped
½ small onion, finely chopped
1½ cups Israeli couscous
1½ cups vegetable stock
1 cup water

To cook the couscous; heat oil in a large saucepan over a medium heat. Add the garlic and onion, sauté until the onion is translucent. Add the couscous and stir well. Add the vegetable stock and water, place the lid on and turn the heat down. Cook for ten minutes until liquid is absorbed and the couscous is cooked through—it should still be firm. Transfer to a large salad bowl and allow to cool.

Salad
2 cups baby snow peas
2 medium sized cucumber, peeled and diced
2 cups cherry tomatoes, halved
3 cups baby spinach, finely sliced
¼ cup fresh coriander leaves, finely chopped
¼ cup fresh mint leaves, finely chopped

Blanch the baby snow peas for 1 minute in boiling water, drain and refresh with cold water. Add the cooled snow peas and rest of the salad ingredients to the cooled couscous. In a separate bowl, place the dressing ingredients and whisk together.

Dressing
¼ cup olive oil
½ lemon, juice and zest
1 tsp Dijon mustard
1 tsp sugar
salt and pepper to taste

Pour the dressing over the salad and toss to combine.

Strawberry and Rhubarb Salad

½ cup hazelnuts, toasted
2 rhubarb stalks, peeled
1 tbsp sugar
1 tbsp fresh orange juice
(or Cointreau)
1 tbsp fresh lemon juice
5 cups of fresh strawberries,
hulled and cut into ¼'s
¼ cup mint leaves, finely sliced

Dry roast the hazelnuts until golden brown, allow to cool and then roughly chop.

Finely slice the rhubarb on the diagonal. Place the rhubarb, sugar, orange juice and lemon juice in a bowl, toss together and leave to marinate for at least 30 minutes. Add the fresh strawberries and mint, toss together and then sprinkle with hazelnuts.

Superfood Salad with Pan-fried Halloumi

Sue Gunn

This salad serves 4 and is packed to the brim with goodness, with lots of fresh super-nutritious vegetables, a creamy avocado dressing, seeds and quinoa. Topped with some golden pan-fried halloumi, it's delicious and will make you feel great!

In a small pot, bring quinoa, water and a good pinch of salt to the boil. As soon as it is boiling, cover with a tight fitting lid and reduce to low heat to cook for 15 minutes. Turn off heat and leave (still covered) to finish steaming for 5 minutes. Remove lid, fluff up grains with a fork and leave to cool slightly.

While quinoa is cooking, prepare the vegetables. Finely slice cos lettuce. Peel and coarsely grate or shred beetroot; peel and coarsely grate or shred carrots; thinly slice radishes. Place all in a bowl, along with sauerkraut, parsley and dates.

Blend all avocado dressing ingredients in a blender until smooth, season to taste with salt and pepper and more lemon juice, if needed. Set aside.

Add quinoa to salad bowl, drizzle with extra-virgin olive oil and lemon juice and gently toss to combine. Season to taste with salt and pepper.

In a small dry fry-pan, toast sunflower seeds on medium heat for about 2 minutes, moving the pan around frequently, until lightly toasted. Set aside.

Heat olive oil in a large non-stick fry-pan on medium heat. Pan-fry halloumi for 1 - 2 minutes on each side until golden.

To serve, divide salad between plates, top with 3 slices halloumi per portion, drizzle with avocado dressing and scatter with toasted sunflower seeds.

½ cup quinoa (white, red or black)
¾ cup water
100 - 120g cos lettuce
1 medium beetroot
2 carrots
3 baby radishes
1 cup sauerkraut
½ cup finely chopped parsley
6 - 8 pitted medjool dates, chopped
1 tsp extra-virgin oil
juice of ½ lemon

Avocado dressing
flesh of ½ avocado
juice of ½ lemon
½ small clove garlic, minced
¼ cup cold water

Halloumi and sunflower seeds
¼ cup sunflower seeds
½ tsp olive oil
200g halloumi, cut into 12 slices

Fettuccine with Smoked Salmon

Serves 3 – 4. This recipe uses fresh, homemade fettuccine however you can also buy fresh spinach fettuccine at your local grocer.

400g fresh spinach fettuccine,
(see recipe below)
2 tbsp olive oil
2 cloves garlic, crushed
300 ml cream
1 spray-free lemon, zest and juice
½ cup Parmesan cheese
2 egg yolks
salt
white pepper
300g hot smoked salmon fillet

Boil the fettuccine in plenty of salted water until just cooked and they still have a very firm 'al dente' centre. Drain, but do not rinse.

While fettuccine are cooking; heat olive oil in a large sauce pan, add garlic. Sauté for 1 minute, you do not want it to colour—add cream, lemon zest and Parmesan cheese, simmer to reduce for a couple of minutes. Add the cooked fettuccine and mix over heat. Remove from heat, add the egg yolks, season with salt and pepper and toss to combine.

Coarsely flake the salmon by hand and fold in gently. Serve in individual bowls with a squeeze of fresh lemon juice.

Spinach Fettuccine

This recipe makes 600g of fresh pasta.

½ bunch of fresh spinach,
approximately 200g
4 tbsp olive oil
400g high grade flour
4 egg yolks
1 whole egg
additional flour for rolling

Cut the roots off the spinach and coarsely chop the stalks and leaves; wash and then dry thoroughly. In a frying-pan, heat the oil until just before smoking point, add the spinach and wilt quickly over a high heat. Remove from the pan and spread out to cool. Squeeze out any remaining liquid from the spinach, place in food processor and process until finely chopped. Add flour and keep on processing a further 3 – 4 minutes. Add the egg and egg yolks, and pulse until the mixture just comes together.

Turn out onto a floured work bench and knead until the dough is smooth and supple and the dough springs back into shape when pressed. Shape the dough into a ball, dust with flour and cover in cling-film, rest for 30 minutes. Roll out the dough in stages, when the dough starts to contract, allow to rest for a short while before rolling again.

Repeat this process until you have a sheet of dough approximately 1 - 2mm thick. Once at the desired thickness, cut into strips. Be sure the strands are the same thickness so that they cook evenly. Toss the fettuccine with your hands, using a dusting of flour to prevent sticking.

Keep in a dry place until ready to be cooked.

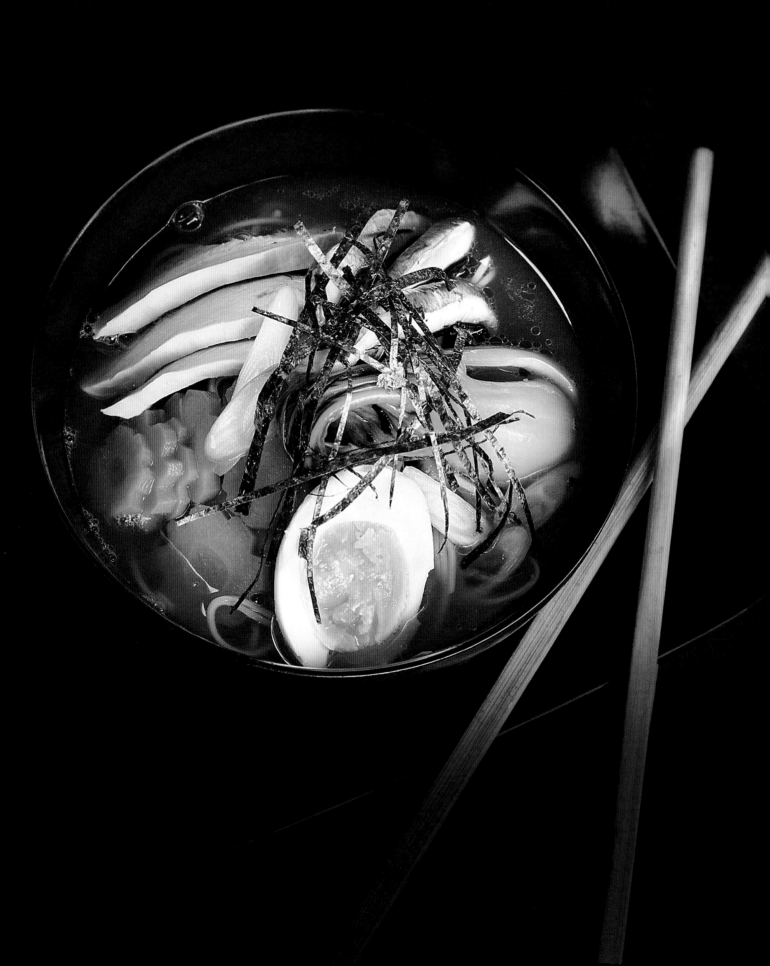

Chicken Ramen Soup

This recipe is sufficient for 4 serves. Ramen is a Japanese style broth with noodles, and the broth can be varied according to taste. If you want a vegetarian meal, use vegetable stock and fried tofu—frying the tofu gives added texture. Other variations include replacing the chicken with pork or beef or adding sake or dashi. This recipe uses home-made chilli oil, the amount 'drizzled' is dependant on your taste buds, but the chilli gives the dish an added lift. If you don't like the heat of the chilli oil, use sesame oil instead.

Place the whole chicken breast in the chicken stock and bring to a simmer, slowly poach the chicken until it is cooked through—approximately 10 minutes. While the chicken is simmering, cook the ramen noodles according to the packet instructions, drain and put to one side. Boil the eggs, you want them semi-soft, around 7 – 8 minutes, drain and place under running cold water.

When the chicken is cooked through, remove and put to one side. Add the carrots, bok choy and mushrooms—simmer until just cooked, do not overcook. If using portobello mushrooms, cook whole and then slice for serving. Remove the vegetables from the stock and place to one side.

Add the ginger, miso paste (this is optional) and soy sauce to the broth and adjust seasonings to taste.

Ramen soup is best served in individual bowls with the ingredients added in layers. Divide the noodles into 4 and place in the centre of each bowl, slice the chicken and arrange on top, then add the vegetables and half an egg. Pour the hot stock over the top and garnish with spring onions and a drizzle of chilli oil.

Finish with the finely sliced nori strips.

1 litre chicken stock
250g chicken breast
200g ramen noodles,
2 eggs
2 medium sized carrots, sliced thinly
2 small bok choy, washed and cut in half
150g fresh shiitake or portobello mushrooms
1 tsp fresh ginger, finely grated
2 – 3 tbsp soy sauce
2 – 3 tbsp miso paste, optional
1 spring onion, sliced on an angle
chilli oil
nori sheet, sliced into thin strips

Chilli Garlic Oil

This oil can be stored in a jar and added to any dish if you desire that extra heat.

In a small saucepan add all the ingredients and slowly heat to about 60° C. Allow to cool down.

1 cup sunflower oil
1 – 2 tsp dried chilli flakes
3 cloves garlic, crushed
5 black pepper corns

Telecommunication cabinets around the city have been painted with artists' impressions from our region. The art includes paintings of some our more famous residents: historian Don Stafford, entertainer Sir Howard Morrison, basketball player Steven Adams, All Black Buck Shelford and Aviator Jean Batten.

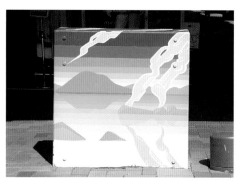

Christina (Tina) Hurihua Wirihina

Ngāti Whaawhaakia Tainui, Ngāti Pikiao, Te Arawa

Tina lives on the shores of Lake Rotoiti, waking up each morning to the view of her maunga (mountain) Matawhaura. A gifted artist, Tina is well-renowned for her beautiful weaving, her projects are inspired by the surrounds and natural resources of her home. Tina's mother, Matekino Lawless (QSM) another renowned weaver, has also been a major influence.

Tina co-ordinated and was one of a collective of artists involved in the creation of 49 turapa tukutuku panels, *Kāhui Raranga: The Art of Tukutuku*, now a permanent installation on the New Zealand Wall at the United Nations Headquarters, a unique statement of New Zealand's national identity.

Parāoa Rēwena

Parāoa Rēwena is a traditional Māori sourdough bread, using fermented potato instead of yeast. Prior to the arrival of Europeans, Māori lived off the land and sea. They were known for having extensive gardens and growing kūmara and taewa, what are now called Māori potatoes, bought with them from Polynesia. These days standard European varieties of potato are more commonly used.

The art of making rēwena is passed down through the generations, Tina was taught by her mother Matekino and in turn she now teaches her grandchildren. The cast iron umu Tina uses was passed down to her by a family friend. Tina's parāoa starts several days earlier with the making of the potato starter, she doesn't use salt in her recipe, the flavour provided by a good starter is sufficient. There is no set recipe, it is all made by feel.

Peel a handful of potatoes or kūmara, cut into small pieces and boil in water until mushy.
Once cool, add ½ cup sugar and then 1 cup of flour.
Leave for several days for the mixture to ferment, the 'starter' can be kept alive with regular feeding of potato water and sugar.
Once the potato has fermented, the parāoa is ready to be made.
Add wholemeal and white flour to the starter, mixing with a fork to combine.
Once it has reached 'gooey' consistency, tip out onto a lightly floured surface
and start to gently knead, adding flour as required.
The dough should be firm but still soft to touch.
When ready, the dough will roll easily around the bench.
Form the dough to the shape of your umu or loaf tin.
Dust lightly with flour before placing inside.
Set aside and allow to rise.
When double in size, place in a cold oven and set the temperature to 220º C.
Bake for 1 - 1½ hours or until baked through.

Boiled Fruitcake

Dave Donaldson
Rotorua Councillor, Deputy Mayor and keen mountain biker

This is my mother's recipe which basically kept me alive through the first months of my Police Cadet training in Trentham Camp [1968-69] and the shock of dining at the Immigration Hostel! I have always loved a moist fruit cake and Mum would send me one of these on a monthly basis, or more frequently if my barracks mates insisted on visiting my sock drawer for a slice!

Now my wife makes it every Christmas and it's a never-fail recipe.

1 can (435g) crushed pineapple
1 pkt (400g) mixed fruit
125g butter
1 cup sugar
1 tsp mixed spice
1 tsp baking soda
2 eggs
1 cup self-raising flour
1 cup plain flour

Put the following ingredients in a saucepan; pineapple, mixed fruit, butter, sugar, mixed spice and baking soda, boil together for 10 minutes.

Allow to cool.

Fold eggs and flour into the cooled mixture. Pour into a prepared cake tin and bake at 160° C for 1 hour.

Chocolate Cream Shortcake

Jill Nicholas

This divine chocolate shortcake also came from the mother's cookbook. It is a recipe given to her by Rona Stephenson, Taupo electorate MP from 1962 - 1983 when she retired, it's hand written on electorate letterhead.

4 oz butter
4 oz sugar
6 oz flour
1 tsp baking powder
1 dsp cocoa

Mix together the top 5 ingredients and press half into a buttered sponge-roll tin.

For topping:
¼ tin sweetened condensed milk
1 oz butter
1 dsp golden syrup

Melt the topping ingredients over hot water and spread over the shortcake base. Crumble the remainder of the cake mix on top and bake for half an hour in a slow oven.

Can be iced with chocolate icing if liked, but not necessary.

Right: Sunrise from Mt Ngongotahā overlooking Lake Rotorua

Focaccia Bread

Steve Chadwick
Mayor of Rotorua

In this life I never have bread at hand so this is handy when family or friends descend. I originally got this recipe from Lois Daish, a New Zealand restaurateur, food writer and cookbook author.

Place flour in a large mixing bowl and mix in salt. Sprinkle the yeast and sugar over the ¼ cup warm water. Stir and set aside for 10 minutes until the mixture is frothy. Make a well in the middle of the flour and pour in the yeast mixture, followed by the rest of the warm water and olive oil. Mix all together with your hands. It should be moister than a typical bread dough, more like a moist scone mixture. Tip out onto a floured board and knead lightly for several minutes. Put back into a clean, oiled bowl and cover with plastic wrap. Put in a warm place until well risen. Depending on the warmth of the day, this will take from 1 to 2 hours. The dough should be light and puffy.

Turn out onto a floured board and divide into two balls. Lightly knead the balls of dough, one at a time. You will find the dough is much less sticky after the first rising, and also easier to handle. After kneading; roll or press out the dough until it is 10 - 15mm thick. Brush two sponge-roll tins or baking dishes with low sides generously with olive oil. Place the dough in the tin and prick all over with a thick-pronged fork. Brush generously with olive oil and sprinkle with coarse salt. Put in a warm place to rise until double the thickness.

Bake in a preheated 225° C oven for about 20 minutes. Lower the heat a little and continue baking for another 10 minutes or so until the focaccia is well browned and crisp. Remove from the oven and immediately brush with more olive oil. Cut into wedges or strips and serve.

500g plain flour
2 tsp salt
¼ cup warm water
1 tsp dried yeast
1 tsp sugar
1 - 1½ cups warm water
2 tbsp olive oil

Seasoning
¼ cup olive oil
salt (preferably coarse sea salt)

Gateau Concorde

Helen Macfarlane

This was one of the most spectacular gateaux I learned to make while attending a class conducted by the head pastry chef from the famed LeNotre patisserie school outside of Paris. My grandson Oliver's favourite dessert and a long term favourite on Poppy's dessert menu, it is chocolate heaven. You can vary the recipe by omitting the cocoa in the meringue and layering the meringues with lemon curd, whipped cream and blueberries or berries of choice. Oliver, however, would consider this sacrilege!

1 cup icing sugar
3 tbsp cocoa powder
5 egg whites
⅔ cup castor sugar

Preheat oven to 150° C. Line baking trays with baking paper. Draw 3x20cm circles, heart shapes or ovals. Sift cocoa powder with icing sugar. Beat egg whites until stiff and gradually add castor sugar, a little at a time until all absorbed and mixture stiff and smooth. Gently fold through sifted icing sugar and cocoa. Fill a piping bag with a 1cm nozzle and fill in drawn shapes. There should be enough meringue over to fill another piping bag with a smaller nozzle to pipe long strips onto baking sheets. Bake in oven for 1 hour. Meringue should not brown, lower heat if they do. Strips should be done earlier so remove from oven. Give shapes a further 10 mins then turn off oven and leave to cool.

Chocolate Mousse
180g dark chocolate
100g butter
3 egg yolks
1 cup cream, whipped
2 tbsp Cointreau or Grand Mariner

Make mousse. Melt chocolate with butter gently and stir in egg yolks with liqueur. Fold through whipped cream and allow to set until firm enough to spread on shapes and sandwich together. Save some mousse to spread on top then break up sticks and pile on top and sides. Dust lightly with icing sugar and decorate with whole strawberries.

Also delicious with a berry purée and served with a dollop of whipped cream.

Hedgehogs

Denise Caudwell

When I first moved to Pukehangi Road 37 years ago, I had a lovely neighbour who would appear each week with delicious home-made baking. This included these hedgehogs. Sadly, my neighbour has since passed away, but I make these lovely biscuits and give them away to friends, who may be unwell or just need cheering up.

8 oz butter
8 oz sugar
2 eggs
4 tbsp milk
1½ cups sultanas
2 cups flour
2 tsp baking powder
pinch salt
cornflakes to roll them in

Cream butter and sugar and gradually add beaten eggs and then the milk and sultanas. Add sifted flour, baking powder and salt, mix evenly. Take teaspoons of the mixture and toss evenly in the cornflakes.

Place on a prepared baking tray lined with baking paper, cook in a moderate oven until lightly brown.

Rhubarb Tart

We have a thriving, dark red-stemmed rhubarb plant in our vegetable garden, given to us by friends several years ago. Each year we eagerly await the first harvest, a signal that spring is finally on its way.

In a food processor, pulse flour, salt, butter, baking powder and sugar together until the mixture is crumble. Don't over mix.

Slowly add (pulse) the egg and vinegar, then dribble in cold water until just combined. Turn out onto a lightly floured surface and form into a ball, it should come together easily and not be sticky. Wrap in clingwrap and place in refrigerator for a minimum of 30 minutes.

Preheat oven to 210° C.

Remove pastry from refrigerator and allow to soften for a few minutes before rolling. On a lightly floured surface roll the pastry out to 3mm thickness and line a 20cm flan tin, preferably with a removable bottom. To blind bake; cover the pastry with baking paper, ensuring the edges are also covered to avoid burning, and fill with dried beans or chickpeas distributed evenly.

Place in centre of oven, reducing temperature to 200° C, and bake for 5 minutes. Remove and allow to cool.

Reduce oven temperature to 180° C.

Cream together the butter and sugar. Add ground almonds. Slowly add egg, egg yolk and finely grated lemon rind. Gently fold in the flour.

Pour almond mixture into the pre-baked tart base and spread the rhubarb pieces over the top. Place in oven, reducing the temperature to 150° C.

Bake until cooked, approximately 20 minutes.

Sweet Short Pastry
225g flour
¼ tsp salt
125g butter
1 tsp baking powder
20g sugar
1 egg
1 tsp cider vinegar

Tart filling
130g butter
130g castor sugar
130g ground almonds
1 egg
1 egg yolk
rind from 1 lemon
20g flour
fresh rhubarb
(peeled and sliced into 1cm pieces)

Overleaf: Champagne Pool, Wai-O-Tapu

Beau Rivage Cream Caramel

Philippa Wills

This recipe comes from my sister Jackie, who shows her love of people through food. It is a favourite because not only does it taste great and really impresses, but it is also dead easy! I think this is just the effect of the individual ramekins and the performance of plating them. Best prepared the day before if possible.

8 ramekins
10 oz sugar
1½ tbsp water
700 mls milk
6 eggs
3 tbsp Grand Marnier
(I have substituted with whatever we have)

Heat half the sugar with the water until it turns brown, then pour the caramel into the ramekins. Boil milk (using the same pot cleans it and adds flavour) then pour it into a bowl with eggs beaten with the remaining sugar. Add 1 tbsp Grand Marnier, fold together and then fill the ramekins.

Place the ramekins in a pan of hot water and bake at 120° C for 20 minutes. Refrigerate. Turn out (may need hot water on the base) and pour Grand Marnier over before serving with cream, fresh oranges/kiwifruit.

Judy's Lemon Cake

Judy Gregor

This recipe has been a family favourite for several years now, not just as a cake but also a good option for dessert. If coconut yoghurt is used, then it is dairy free. A food processor means it is a doddle to make.

1¾ cup sugar
rind of 2 lemons
2 eggs
1 cup oil, I use a vegetable oil but not avocado
½ tsp salt
1 cup yoghurt - plain or lemon flavoured
or coconut for a dairy free option
2 - 3 tbsp lemon juice
2 cups self-raising flour

Line and grease 25cm cake tin. Set fan bake oven to 180° C. When measuring the flour, spoon it into the cup from the packet. Do not pack it down or press it in.

Using a food processor put the sugar into the bowl, peel the lemons with a potato peeler and blitz the two together until the peel is finely distributed throughout the sugar. Add eggs, oil and salt and process until thick and smooth. Add yoghurt and lemon juice and blend enough to mix. Add the flour and process just enough to combine the flour with the rest of the mixture. Pour into the prepared tin. Bake for 45 minutes (though may take a little longer), until cooked and a skewer comes out clean. Leave to cool for 10 minutes or so before turning out onto a rack. Serve plain or with cream and/or yoghurt.

If making in a bowl, grate the lemons and beat with the oil, eggs and sugar before adding the remaining ingredients as listed.

Right: Rotorua Centennial Park

Joy's Quick Golden Dumplings

Tricia Vickers

In the 1970's I was living on a dairy farm at Rerewhakaaitu. My parents were visiting at the time and I was making dessert. Dad said he wouldn't have any as he didn't like sweet things......however he decided to taste the orange sauce AND he was hooked!

Rub butter into flour, add baking powder and salt. Add milk and quickly form a soft dough. Gently pat into 8 dumplings with lightly floured hands.

Dumplings
1 cup flour
50g butter
1 heaped tsp baking powder
pinch of salt
½ cup milk (or a little more)

Mix all ingredients in a large saucepan. Bring to the boil then drop dumplings in. Turn heat down to a simmer, put lid on pan and cook for 20 minutes approximately before checking.

Delicious served with vanilla ice cream!!

Orange Sauce
1 tbsp golden syrup
½ cup sugar
1 cup water
rind (finely grated) and juice of an orange
pinch of salt

Pavlina

Lorraine Hutt

Decadent. I looked the word decadent up in the dictionary and one, and only one, of its meanings is self-indulgent—the others are not very nice indeed!

Preheat oven to 175° C.

Beat the egg whites until stiff, add the sugar and beat again. Sprinkle a sheet of baking paper with castor sugar, spread out the meringue to approximately ½ inch thick and sprinkle with coconut. Bake for 8 – 10 minutes. Remove and leave to cool. When cold, flip onto a tea towel and spread with whipped cream, berries or passion fruit.

Roll up like a Swiss role—care needs to be taken with this step.

4 egg whites
¾ cup castor sugar
coconut
passion fruit pulp or berries
cream, whipped

Traditional Scones

Jo Nicholson

Home baking, there is nothing quite like a traditional afternoon tea of fresh pikelets or scones straight from the pan or oven, served with whipped cream and jam.

Preheat oven to 200º C.

Place the flour and salt in a large mixing bowl and form a well in the centre. Pour in the cream and lemonade (make sure it has not gone flat) and mix together, you want a soft dough.

Tip onto a clean, lightly floured bench top and using your hands, gently form a square of dough of around 2cm thick. Cut into approximately 12 even pieces and place onto a prepared baking tray.

Bake for 10 – 12 minutes or until golden brown.

4 cups self-raising flour
pinch of salt
300 ml can lemonade
300 ml fresh cream

Aunty Joan Shepherd's Pikelets

Jo Nicholson

Separate 1 egg, beat the white stiff, add the yolk and gradually add ½ cup of sugar. Beat until creamy. Dissolve ½ tsp of soda in 1 cup milk and add. Then add 1 good cup of flour, 1 large tsp baking powder and a pinch of salt. Melt together 1 tsp golden syrup and 1 dessert spoon of butter and add to the mixture. Leave the mixture to stand for a while before using.

Heat a lightly buttered non-stick pan on a medium heat. Drop dessert spoonsful of the mixture into the pan. When the pikelets bubble, turn and cook the other side. Remove from pan and keep warm in a clean tea towel.

Jam Sandwich

Mary Barton

Growing up in the austerity of war-torn Britain, Mary Barton learnt her culinary skills at a finishing school specialising in instructing pupils on the art of becoming "good little wives". This recipe comes direct from the pages of *The Glasgow Cookery Book's 16th edition;* a publication compiled especially for students in training. Introductory Scullery Work (sic) notes provide an extensive course in the art of washing up. Turn to the meat section and the grizzly instructions for roasting a fowl, begin with plucking and singeing, before beheading it and extracting its gizzard—that's just for starters.

This less labour intensive and more contemporary-relevant recipe is reproduced exactly as it appears.

3 oz flour
3 oz sugar
½ tsp baking powder
2 eggs
1½ oz butter
some jam

Sift flour, after drying if necessary. Beat eggs and sugar until light and frothy, stir in melted butter, gradually add flour and baking powder, mixing lightly.

Turn into prepared tin and bake in a fairly hot oven for 10 minutes if in two tins, about 15 minutes if in one tin. When cold split open, spread with jam and sift sugar on top.

Still a favourite from Mary's kitchen, she sometimes swaps the jam for lemon juice and fills with lemon curd.

Best Big Fat Chewy Chocolate Chip Cookies

Jenny Eaves

From a very good friend of mine (with lots of grandchildren)!

Heat oven to 160° C. Line trays with baking paper.

Sift dry ingredients. Cream butter and sugars, add vanilla and egg, plus egg yolk. Fold the dry ingredients into the creamed mixture, and then add in chocolate chips and fold again. Put small spoonful's 8 cm apart onto baking tray, they spread a lot. Bake for 10 - 15 mins, don't overcook.

Take out of the oven while still very light brown—this ensures a chewy texture.

250g plain flour
2g baking soda
3g salt
170g butter, softened
100g white sugar
220g brown sugar
15 ml vanilla
1 egg plus 1 egg yolk
335 gm dark block chocolate, broken roughly

Chocolate Ginger Cookies

Anne Foale
Now a proud Kiwi

I am constantly asked for this recipe.

Preheat oven to 180° C and line 2 – 3 baking trays. Cream butter and sugar until pale and fluffy, add egg and vanilla, beat well.

Gently fold in sifted flour, ground ginger and salt. Add walnuts, chocolate chips and chopped ginger, stirring until combined. Roll tablespoons of the mixture into balls and place on baking trays, about 6cm apart as they spread.

Bake for 12 – 14 minutes, cool on trays for 5 minutes before transferring to a wire rack.

Suitable to freeze.

185g unsalted butter
250g castor sugar
½ tsp vanilla extract
1 egg
300g self-raising flour
2 tsp ground ginger
¼ tsp salt
100g walnut halves, toasted and chopped
200g dark chocolate bits
200g chopped ginger

Left: Wisteria covered bridge, Kuirau Park

Carmelitas

Heather Vail

My kids' favourite ooey-gooey layered bar, makes approximately 20 bars.

50 soft caramel candies
⅓ cup+, evaporated milk
1 cup flour
1 cup quick-cooking oatmeal
¾ cup brown sugar
1 tsp baking soda
pinch of salt
¾ cup melted butter
1 cup chocolate chips
(semi-sweet or your favourite mix!)
1 cup chopped pecans

Preheat the oven to 175° C and butter a large baking pan (33x22x5cm).

Unwrap caramels and put in saucepan with milk; heat on low burner and stir constantly until thick and creamy. Set aside.

Make the bottom streusel layer: combine flour, oatmeal, sugar, soda and salt. Beat in melted butter. Press half the streusel into the baking pan and bake for ten minutes. Remove from oven and rest a minute.

Drizzle streusel with most of the melted caramel; reserve some. Sprinkle on the chocolate chips and pecans. Layer on the remaining streusel dough (do not press). Bake 15 minutes.

Remove from oven and drizzle with remaining caramel.

It's best to refrigerate Carmelitas for a few hours before slicing to serve.

Grandmother's Shortbread

Fay Olphert

Many people who ask for this recipe are the 'husbands'—don't ask me why.

1 lb butter
1½ cups sugar
1 small pinch salt
4 heaped cups of flour
2 tbsp cornflour

Take out two large tablespoons of flour and replace with two tablespoons of cornflour.

Mix butter, sugar and salt well together (I use Kenwood cake mixer and mix for 15 minutes). Then add sifted flours.

Knead for a few minutes and then roll out on bench or large floured board. Cut into the shapes you desire and prick with a fork.

Bake in slow oven (about 140º C) in middle of oven for about ¾ - 1 hour, depending on how hot your oven is. Should be cream in colour. You can tell if cooked if you look at the underside as shortbread should not be a fawn colour which can easily happen if overcooked.

Right: Annika, aged 2½ years

Diwali Festival

Rotorua has a large and active Indian community, comprising of a very wide variety of nationalities and religions. Some are new residents to New Zealand but many of the families have been here for generations. This community have successfully managed to navigate themselves and their families into a Kiwi way of life while maintaining and celebrating the culture and religious beliefs of their heritage. Festivals such as Diwali (The Festival of Lights) have become a feature enjoyed and celebrated by the diverse Rotorua community.

Indian Seasoning

Ruth Gadgil

Peter Gadgil, eminent New Zealand Forest Pathologist, was born in Poona, Maharashtra, India. After living in England and Wales he finally settled in Rotorua. He was more interested in English than Indian culture but retained one basic Indian element in his cooking repertoire. This involved use of Asa foetida, better known in Indian English as hing.

Hing has been described as a repulsively-smelling gum-resin, used in every classical kitchen. The aroma is certainly offensive, but also strangely attractive. It is also considered to have valuable medicinal properties.

This is the way that Peter Gadgil used hing in his curries:
Cover the bottom of a saucepan with cooking oil. When hot, add ½ tsp of mustard seed and then a pinch of freshly-ground hing. Cover the pan and fry the contents until brown (the seeds will pop as they heat). Add chopped onion, fry for a while, then add water and boil until cooked.

This forms a base for many dishes. Peter liked to mix it with cooked peas or beans. He also made a very hot pickle by adding salt, dry mustard, lemon juice, chopped root ginger and chopped hot chillies. This keeps well—but use with caution!

Patel Family

Shash and Achla Patel along with their three daughters, Shivani, Priya and Nishali are a close family who live successfully within both cultures. Both Achla and Shash are very active in the Rotorua community; through their work, their daughter's extra-curricular activities, as community volunteers and also in their involvement with the BOP (Rotorua) Indian Association.

The Patel's are vegetarians and these Gujarati recipes are those that Achla has learnt from her mother. The family eat western style food 3 - 4 times a week and Indian food 2 - 3 times a week. Please note: a word from the girls at the photo shoot—they don't dress and eat like this every day!

Left: Achla, Shivani, Shash, Priya, Nishali

Paratha

Achla Patel

Paratha is unleavened flat bread; this bread is more substantial than chapattis as it is layered by repeatedly brushing with ghee and folding. The bread is then cooked on a hot tarvi, a circular, slightly concave iron pan.

3 cups chapatti or wholemeal flour
1 cup white flour
salt
4 tbsp oil
ghee

Mix together the two flours and salt. Make a well in the middle and slowly add the oil, mixing by hand to form a soft dough. Allow to rest for a few minutes. Portion into balls, coat the ball of dough in flour and flatten with the palm of your hand onto the board, this helps to obtain the needed round shape. Use a circular board as your template and roll out, rotating consistently to keep the round shape and adding flour to stop it sticking.

Brush with warmed ghee and fold in half, and then half again, making it a triangle. Roll out to about 3mm thickness.

Place in the hot tarvi or flat pan, turn over to cook both sides. Brush with ghee.

Potato and Cauliflower Curry

Achla Patel

We like the vegetables to be well cooked and soft, but if you prefer you can keep them crunchier. Add peas if you wish.

2 - 3 tbsp oil
2 tsp cumin seeds
2 medium potatoes, cut into small cubes
1 cauliflower, cut into small florets
salt
lela masala (green chilli) crushed
1 tsp turmeric
2 tsp ground cumin and coriander
1 large fresh tomato, diced finely
fresh coriander leaves, chopped

Heat oil in a large pan. Add cumin seeds and allow to infuse. Add the potato and cauliflower and the rest of the spices. Stir through and place lid on pan and cook slowly. When cooked to your liking add the fresh tomato and stir through.

Just before serving, stir through the fresh, chopped coriander leaves.

Sweetcorn Handvo

Achla Patel

Handvo is a traditional Gujarati savory cake, this one is made with creamed corn. It keeps well in an airtight container.

Heat oil in a small pan and add the mustard seeds, cumin and sesame seeds, allow to infuse and pop and then put to one side to cool.

Mix lightly together by hand the flours, semolina and oil. Add the corn, salt, baking powder, ginger, chilli, coriander and turmeric.

Add natural yogurt and some water, mixing until you have a thick and runny batter, add the eno.

Spread half the cooled seeds and oil over the base of an oblong cake tin or deep baking tray. Pour in the batter. Spread over the top the rest of the seeds and smooth over.

Bake in the over at 180° C for 20 - 30 minutes. Once baked, place under the grill for a few minutes to brown the top. Cut into squares to serve.

2 tbsp oil
1 tsp rai (mustard seeds)
2 tsp cumin
tul (sesame seeds)
½ cup chana atta (chickpea flour)
½ cup white flour
1 cup semolina
1 tbsp oil
1 can creamed corn
salt
1 tsp baking powder
fresh ginger, grated
lela masala (green chilli) crushed
lela dhana (coriander)
tumeric
yogurt
water
1 level tsp eno

Aubergine and Potato Curry

Achla Patel

Heat oil in large pan, add vegetables and spices. Place lid on and cook slowly until vegetables are tender.

1 aubergine, sliced into rounds
2 medium potatoes, sliced in rounds
4 - 5 tbsp oil
salt
lela masala (green chilli) crushed
½ tsp turmeric
3 tsp ground cumin and coriander

Summer

Chickpea Nuggets with Chargrilled Salad

Chickpea Nuggets
1 cup dried chickpeas
soaked in water overnight
1 small onion
2 cloves garlic
zest of 1 lemon
½ tsp turmeric
salt
ground white pepper
3 tbsp fresh mint, chopped
2 tbsp cornflour or chickpea flour
oil for frying

Peel and chop onion and garlic and place in food processor, pulse 2 - 3 times.

Add the rest of the ingredients and process to a coarse paste. Cover with clingfilm and place in the fridge for 30 minutes before cooking.

Take a spoonful at a time and form small patties, cook on the barbecue hotplate or in a frying pan.

Salad
4 medium courgettes, sliced on angle
3 medium red peppers, cut into wedges
2 cups snow peas
1 bunch baby carrots, scrubbed
mixture of fresh lettuce leaves
fresh basil leaves to garnish
balsamic vinegar
olive oil

Season vegetables with salt and pepper and chargrill.

To assemble salad; arrange platter with mixed lettuce leaves, chargrilled vegetables and chickpea patties. Garnish with fresh basil and drizzle with balsamic vinegar and olive oil just before serving.

Roasted Red Pepper Pesto

Joanne Bryant

This is a great recipe if you have guests who are either vegan or celiac. Serve with crostini or rice crackers. Alternatively, add a little more oil and toss together with your favourite pasta.

2 red peppers, roasted
1 cup fresh Italian or flat leaf parsley
½ cup fresh basil
2 - 3 cloves garlic
½ cup capers or green olives
4 tbsp blanched almonds
⅓ cup olive oil
2 tbsp white wine vinegar

Process the first 6 ingredients together in a food processor. Slowly add oil and vinegar until you have the right consistency.

Basil Pesto

2 cups finely chopped fresh basil leaves
1 cup roasted cashews nuts
1 clove garlic, crushed
¼ cup freshly grated parmesan cheese
lemon juice
salt
white pepper
¾ cup olive oil (adjust as necessary)

Place all ingredients in a blender and pulse to a coarse paste, adjust seasoning and oil as required.

Charred Capsicum Salsa

1 whole small garlic
5 medium sized red and yellow capsicums
3 - 5 medium sized red chillies
salt and pepper
1 tbsp balsamic vinegar
2 tbsp olive oil
1 red onion

Cut the garlic in half, cross wise. Char the peppers, chillies and garlic over an open flame until they are blackened and the skin blisters. While still hot, place the chillies and peppers in a bowl and cover with clingfilm. Allow to cool. Peel the blistered skin off, remove seeds, and dice.

Squeeze the garlic from the skin into a mortar, add salt and pepper and using the pestle, grind to a paste.

Add oil and vinegar and combine. Add the rest of the ingredients and stir to combine.

Pa's Plum Sauce

2 kg plums, stones out and cut into pieces
1 tsp ground ginger
2 tsp salt
500g sugar
3 peppercorns
3 cloves garlic, crushed
400 ml malt or cider vinegar
cayenne pepper to taste

Place all ingredients (other than the cayenne
pepper), into a large pot and bring to the boil.

Simmer until plums are soft and then strain
through a colander. Add a pinch of cayenne
pepper to taste.

Tzatziki

1½ cups of plain Greek yogurt
1 cup diced cucumber
lemon juice to taste
2 tsp chopped dill
salt
white pepper

Combine all the ingredients just before serving.

Nabih Mansur

Palestinian born Nabih is a regular at the Thursday night market—a line quickly forms for those wanting his well-known falafel for dinner. The food market is where, together with his wife Cate (a kiwi), he is able to share the food of his childhood.

Nabih was only 6 months old when his family were forced to flee their home and thriving olive grove, losing all their possessions. He has lived most of his life as a refugee (Beirut, Abhu Dhabi) and is now a proud Palestinian/New Zealander and Rotorua resident.

Having made Rotorua their home, the couple participate in many community groups, including volunteering for Hospice and Age Concern.

When Nabih is cooking, he is in his 'happy' place, the recipes of his homeland are known off by heart. For him cooking is a labour of love and the food he creates is an important link to his culture.

Mana'eesh

Nabih Mansur

Mana'eesh is an Arabic flat bread. Topped with Za'atar, dipped in olive oil, Labneh or hummus (recipes below), this is a Palestinian favourite, eaten for breakfast straight from the oven. In previous times, before families had their own home ovens, the village women would take their bread to the local communal ovens to be baked.

1½ tsp active dry yeast
1 tbsp white sugar
1 cup warm water
3 cups bread flour
⅓ cup sunflower oil
1 tsp salt

In a large bowl, combine the yeast, sugar and ½ cup of warm water. The water should not be too hot or the yeast will not proof. Mix together and set aside for about 10 minutes until foamy.

Add the flour, remaining water and salt to the proofed yeast. Knead, slowly adding the oil. If the dough is sticky, add more flour—a tablespoon at a time.

Lightly flour a bowl and place the dough ball inside. Cover with a kitchen towel and let rise in a warm area for an hour, until doubled in size. After an hour or so, divide the dough into 12 balls. Re-cover with the towel and let rise for an additional 30 - 45 minutes.

Preheat the oven to 220° C.

On a floured surface, roll out each dough ball into circles, 6 inches in diameter. Place on a prepared baking sheet. Add together za'atar and olive oil and smear on top of bread, leaving a little bit of room on the edges for spreading (like a pizza).

Bake until brown—10 - 12 minutes.

Za'atar

Nabih Mansur

Za'atar is a mix of herbs that Palestinians use in many ways, on breads such as the Mana'eesh or as a dukkha. It is a symbol of Palestinian cuisine and also of their culture. Wild thyme is extremely resilient, as are the Palestinians who hold onto their cultural roots through their food. You can purchase Sumac at some supermarkets and European style food stores, or just use grated lemon zest instead. Sprinkle Za'atar on bread, mix with olive oil as a dressing or use as a dip. This recipe is extremely versatile.

Briefly process the thyme in a food processor into small pieces, but not a paste. Add the sesame seeds, sumac and salt and mix together with a wooden spoon. Za'atar can be stored in an airtight container for several months.

4 tbsp dried thyme
(home grown and dried is best)
3 tbsp toasted sesame seeds
(use more if you wish)
1½ tsp Sumac
1 tsp salt

Hummus

Nabih Mansur

Boil the chickpeas until soft. Drain and leave to cool briefly before putting them in the blender.

Blend until smooth like peanut butter—about 5 minutes. Add tahini and lemon juice and blend together. Add salt to taste. Hummus freezes well.

chickpeas
(that have been soaked in cold water overnight)
juice from 2 lemons
tahini
sea salt

Labneh

Nabih Mansur

Mix the yoghurt and salt. Put the yoghurt into a muslin covered sieve, that has been placed over a bowl.

Leave overnight or until all the liquid has drained away. You should now have a thick creamy mixture.

Roll the labneh into golf ball size balls. It is now ready to eat as a spread or dip. You can keep it for up to 6 days in the fridge or for up to one year stored in an airtight jar covered with olive oil.

natural yoghurt
sea salt
olive oil (for storage)

Baked Kebab wrapped in Aubergine

Dr Sosek Simonian

My husband Mazen and I immigrated to New Zealand from Iraq in the 1996, and after staying in Auckland for a year, we settled with our family in Rotorua. Sadly, the country we called home and where we grew up, is no longer the country we used to know, having been torn apart by war. Our family enjoys the connection with our culture that food brings, although our recipes can be complicated and take time to make. This recipe is a family favourite taken from *The Iraqi Cookbook* by Lamees Ibrahim and is best served with rice.

Kebabs
450g minced meat
handful of parsley, finely chopped
1 clove garlic, pressed
salt
black pepper
1 tbsp flour or breadcrumbs

Other ingredients
2 large aubergines, sliced lengthways into 16 - 18 slices
700g chopped tomatoes
3 tbsp tomato puree or 500g passata
1 green pepper, sliced
handful of fresh parsley or coriander, chopped
mixed spices, garam masala
salt and black pepper to taste

Prepare the kebab mixture by combining the ingredients, add a little water and knead together. Make finger-shape kebabs and grill or fry as preferred.

Slice the aubergine longitudinally, thinly enough to wrap around the kebabs.

Soak the aubergine slices in brine for an hour, wash in plenty of cold water, drain and dry, then fry lightly to soften (don't let them crisp). Wrap the cooked kebabs with the fried slices of aubergine and line them in a greased oven dish, place a slice of tomato and/or a slice of green pepper in between the kebabs until the dish is full.

Prepare the diluted tomato puree by adding 2 cups of water to the puree or 1 cup to the passata. Add a little salt, spices and black pepper, and pour over. Sprinkle with half the chopped parsley/coriander.

Bake in a hot oven 200º C for 30 minutes.

Garnish with the rest of the parsley/coriander and serve with rice and yogurt with mint or garlic.

Grilled Lamb Fillet Salad

Diana Edwards

120g currants
2 tbsp balsamic vinegar
70g pine nuts
3 tsp olive oil
juice of 1 lemon
4 lamb fillets (rump)
salt and pepper to season
1 radicchio, torn into pieces
200g green beans, blanched
3 small cos leaves
3 cups of rocket leaves
mint

Soak currants in balsamic vinegar for ½ hour. Toss pine nuts in hot pan and roast until golden. Add to marinated currants with olive oil and lemon juice. Set aside to use as the dressing.

Season lamb fillets with salt and pepper and grill until medium rare. Allow to rest.

Mix together the radicchio, beans, cos lettuce, rocket leaves and mint. Slice lamb fillets diagonally and toss together with salad.

Drizzle with currant dressing. Enjoy.

Right: Public art

Christmas Parade

In many towns and cities around the country the annual Christmas parade is a much anticipated event. The city of Rotorua is no exception; local businesses, schools and kindergartens as well as representatives from the ethnic communities get together and provide free entertainment and Christmas themed activities for the children. Colourful and innovative floats, happy children, dance, music and singing, finishing with the appearance of the most important of persons, a smiling Father Christmas. A family orientated day filled with a wonderful air of anticipation and excitement.

Christmas Morning Blueberry French Toast Bake

Heather Vail

On Christmas Eve I put this together and let it rest in the fridge overnight. Christmas morning, I let it bake while our family opens our stockings, and we soon begin to smell the warm aroma—so delicious and easy! The recipe has been adapted from a recipe by Pamela Jaeger in her book *Christmas Pantry*.

Place brown sugar, butter and maple syrup into a saucepan and stir over a gentle heat until thickened. Scrape out into a large baking dish.

In a large bowl beat together; eggs milk, vanilla and salt. Toss in the bread slices to soak. Combine the sugar, cinnamon and nutmeg (spice mix).

Layer evenly in the baking dish: pecans, half the bread slices lifted from the egg mixture, sliced cream cheese, blueberries, spice mix, remaining bread slices and then pour the egg mixture over.

Cover and refrigerate overnight. Remove from fridge and allow to rest for 30 minutes at room temperature. Heat oven to 175° Fahrenheit. Bake uncovered for 1 hour, remove and allow to rest.

Cut into squares and serve upside down, ladle with some maple syrup and serve with a drizzle of yogurt or cream.

1 cup brown sugar
½ cup butter
2 tbsp maple syrup
6 eggs
2 cups milk
2 tsp vanilla extract
pinch of salt
1.5 Italian thin bread loafs
(cut into round, 1cm slices)
1 cup pecan nuts, chopped
½ cup cream cheese
3 cups blueberries
1 cup sugar
2 tsp cinnamon
1 tsp nutmeg

Red Wine Sushi

Takehiro Iwata

Serves 10. I first came to Rotorua in 2008 and am very happy here. I initially trained in French cuisine back in Japan and also had my own restaurant there. This special sushi recipe uses red wine. I make this special sushi on a celebration day, such as when my friends visit Rotorua or a family birthday. The recipe is suitable for vegans and is also gluten free.

Sushi vinegar
¼ cup dark red wine,
(Merlot or Cabernet Sauvignon)
½ cup vinegar
⅓ cup sugar
1 tbsp salt

Put all ingredients in a pan and bring to the boil then set aside.

Vegetables/Filling
Combine colors such as: broccoli cauliflower, beetroot, capsicums, eggs etc

Cut your favourite vegetables into 5mm dices and boil until softened. Mix the cooked vegetables with ⅓ cup of the sushi vinegar.

Sushi rice
3 cups rice, medium or short grain.

Rinse rice and soak it in water for around 1 hour. Cook the rice according to the instruction manual of the rice cooker. Mix cooked rice with the remainder of the sushi vinegar and set aside.

To make the sushi:
1. Make a ring 3cm high with an empty plastic bottle.
3. Put sushi rice into ring until 2cm high, put vegetables on it, hold it and remove the ring.

Topped with Nori seaweed, ham or seafood would also be delicious.

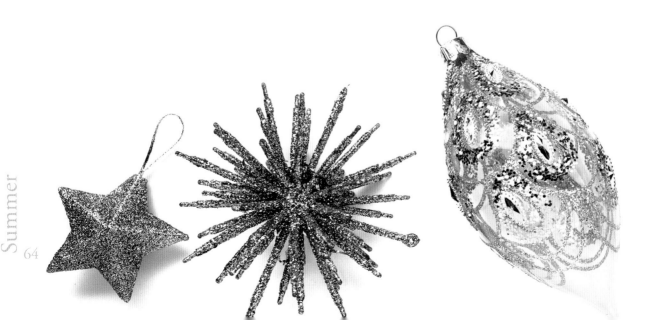

Festive Salmon

Serves 4 - 6. This is a celebration meal, baked salmon fillets topped with fish mousse and served with saffron butter. The recipe uses karengo, a red seaweed considered a delicacy by Māori and which is closely related to Japanese nori. Use nori sheets if you are unable to source the karengo.

For the preparation of the mousse, the ingredients must be kept very cold. So to start, place the fish pieces, cream and whole egg into the deepfreeze until nearly frozen. This will aid in the fish absorbing the cream.

Place the chilled fish, egg, lemon rind and juice, salt and pepper in a cold blender and blend quickly to a paste. Slowly pour in the chilled cream while continuing to blend, combining it into a fine mousse. Check the seasoning and refrigerate.

Pre-heat oven to 200º C. Butter a heat-proof oven dish, one just big enough to fit the salmon fillet in. Cover the bottom with the sliced onion.

Sprinkle the salmon with salt and then brush with egg white. Cover the salmon with karengo sheets and brush again with egg white. Evenly spread the fish mousse over the karengo, approximately 2 – 3cm thick. Gently place the salmon on top of the onion and pour in the sparkling wine (pour in from the side and not over the salmon). Bake in the oven for 25 – 30 minutes, until the salmon is just cooked, be careful not to overcook it.

Place the vermouth, sparkling wine and saffron in a pan and reduce over a medium heat by about a half. Turn up the heat and whisk the cold butter cubes in, one at a time.

To serve, cut the salmon into portion sizes and serve with saffron butter.

Fish Mousse
400g white fish fillets, i.e gurnard or terakihi cut into small pieces
1 egg
300 ml cream
1 lemon, rind
½ lemon, juice
salt
white pepper

Salmon
700g salmon fillet, skin and pin bones removed
knob of butter
1 onion, finely sliced
salt
1 egg white
2 - 3 karengo sheets
500ml dry white wine

Saffron Butter
50 ml dry vermouth
50 ml sparkling wine
pinch saffron
80g butter, cut into cubes

Summer

Beef Fillet Grand Marnier

This is a festive dish, something to cook for that special occasion; Christmas perhaps if you are wanting a change from traditional turkey or ham. Grand Marnier Cordon Rouge was originally created in 1880 by Louis-Alexandre Marnier Laposolle. The orange flavours are enhanced with Cognac and then slowly aged in French oak casks. In cooking, this liqueur is usually associated with desserts, however when used in a meat dish the nuances of orange and hazelnut add a lovely depth of flavour.

Pre-heat oven to 220° C.

Season the fillet with salt and pepper, then brush with mustard. On a piece of cling-film lay the bacon flat, slightly overlapping. Place the seasoned beef on top and roll up, tie together with butchers string. In a heavy-bottomed oven-proof pan, heat the oil to a smoking heat and sear the fillet on all sides. Remove the fillet, place to one side and drain the oil.

Return the pan to a medium heat. Sauté the onions in butter until translucent, add the mushrooms, thyme, and ham and sauté a further 1 – 2 minutes. Add the Grand Marnier and brandy and flambé.

Add the beef stock and crème fraîche, return the fillet to the pan and bake in a pre-heated oven for approximately 20 minutes, turning once.

Rest the meat before slicing and adjust the seasoning of the sauce if required.

1.2 kg beef fillet, trimmed
salt and freshly ground pepper
3 tbsp Dijon mustard
8 – 10 rashers of streaky bacon
2 tbsp vegetable oil

Sauce
1 tbsp butter
½ onion, finely diced
½ cup sliced white button mushrooms
1 cup peeled and sliced brown mushrooms
1 tbsp fresh thyme, rubbed
½ cup ham off the bone, cut into strips
¼ cup Grand Marnier
¼ cup brandy
1 cup brown beef stock
¼ cup crème fraîche

Christmas Cheer

Jill Nicholas

My parents weren't big drinkers but this lethal sounding cocktail was as traditional on Christmas Day as the home reared turkey (shot by my farmer dad of course). I have the retro cocktail glasses in which this pre-dinner drink was served, plus the silver shaker used to blend it. A maraschino cherry on a plastic sword-shaped swizzle stick was a seemingly compulsory add on.

This is exactly how my father recorded it in mum's recipe book—his only offering.

And, no I haven't missed out the ingredients' quantities, none have been left for posterity so use your judgement depending on how festive you feel.

Gin
Sweet and dry vermouth
Dash maraschino liqueur
Small dash bitters
Shake over plenty of ice

Iri's Pavlova

Iri Te Kowhai

Iri was in charge of the catering on the marae at Ōhinemutu, often cooking for hundreds, and sometimes even thousands at a time. This pavlova recipe was one she gave us for the first *Volcanic Kitchens* book in which she featured. Iri has since passed away, her mantra was " I don't write recipes down, I'm a slapper, I slap them together!". Iri's legacy remains, there are many different pavlova recipes around, but this is always our go-to recipe, it never fails.

8 egg whites
2 cups castor sugar
1 dsp spoon vanilla essence
1 dsp spoon vinegar

Preheat oven to 150° C.

Prepare a baking tray lined with baking paper. Beat all the ingredients together at high speed, whisking until very stiff. Spread the meringue onto the baking tray in a 25cm shaped disc. Place in the oven and bake for 30 minutes, reduce temperature to 100° C and continue baking for 1 hour. Turn the oven off and leave the pavlova to cool in the oven with the door shut.

To serve; cover with freshly whipped cream and decorate with fresh fruit—berries, kiwifruit and passionfruit are best.

10/10 Dessert

Joanne Bryant

I got this recipe from a friend of a friend, Freddy at the time was the owner/chef of Morton Estate Restaurant and was known for his amazing desserts. Great for potluck dinners and large group gatherings. I nearly always make it at Christmas when the house is full of people!

210g almonds
350g dark chocolate
200g dried dates or cranberries
5 egg whites
½ cup of castor sugar

Chop finely by hand and mix together the almonds, chocolate and dates/cranberries. Beat the egg whites and sugar until stiff. Fold together in a foil lined cake tin and bake for 40 mins at 180° C. Refrigerate overnight.

Decorate with whipped cream, strawberries, nuts and chocolate and serve in slices.

Chocolate Explosion Cake

Joanne Bryant

Another great, decadent dessert for a large group, serves 15 - 20 people.

Meringue
2 cups of egg whites – approximately 12 eggs
5 cups sugar
pinch salt
1 tbsp cocoa

Filling
1½ litre cream
castor sugar to taste
½ cup cocoa
1 cup toasted, chopped hazelnuts
1 cup dark chocolate buttons
dark chocolate, melted for decoration

Beat together the egg whites, sugar and salt until the mixture is stiff. Fold in the cocoa.

Line oven trays with greaseproof paper. Spread mixture out into 3 x 25cm rounds, approximately 2 - 3cm high. Bake at 90° C for 10 - 12 hours. Remove from oven and allow to cool.

To make the filling; whip the 1½ ltr cream and sweeten with castor sugar to taste. Add cocoa, hazelnuts and chocolate buttons. Set to one side a ¼ of the filling mixture, spread the remaining mixture on one of the meringue rounds and place the second round on top.

Roughly chop the remaining meringue into 2cm pieces and together with the left-over cream mixture, spread over the top and side of the cake. Dribble with dark, melted chocolate.

Angel Cloud Pie

Helen Macfarlane

This recipe is gluten-free and serves 8. Helen attended the La Varenne cooking school in Paris. Together with her late husband, Don, a retired army colonel, they were to open Rotorua's first fine dining establishment, Poppy's in Marguerita St which they had for at least 10 years.

Pie Crust
1 egg white
2 tbsp castor sugar
1 cup+ shredded coconut

Filling
4 level tbsp cornflour
¾ cup sugar
1½ cups boiling water
¼ tsp salt
3 egg whites
3 tbsp castor sugar
1 tsp vanilla essence
½ tsp almond essence
fresh strawberries, raspberies or cherries
whipped cream and chocolate curls

To make the pie crust. Whip egg white until soft peaks form. Gradually beat in castor sugar, beating until stiff. Fold through enough coconut to form a stiff paste. Press into greased 25cm pie dish and bake in 150° C oven for approximately 15 mins or until lightly golden brown.

Filling: Mix cornflour and sugar in saucepan. Add boiling water, stirring constantly until thick and clear (approximately 10 - 12 mins). Add salt to egg whites and whip until stiff. Add remaining sugar gradually with essences until mixture thick and creamy. Pour hot cornflour mixture slowly over meringue mixture, beating continuously and then pour into cooled crust. When cool, top with fresh berries, whipped cream and chocolate curls. If using bottled cherries, drain and thicken juice with 2 tsp cornflour, adding to cherries and cover pie topping with cream swirls and chocolate curls.

Kiwi Christmas Pudding

Marie Raymond

This is a quick, easy and delicious alternative to the traditional Christmas pudding. The recipe was given to me by a friend when I was stressing over the menu for a family Christmas dinner party. It became a family favourite and looks great decorated with New Zealand cherries and kiwifruit.

Put first 6 ingredients into a saucepan, bring to the boil, then simmer over a low heat for 3 - 5 minutes. Add sugar and butter, then cornflour mixed with ¼ cup water. Bring mixture to the boil and stir, remove from the heat.

Put to one side to cool, then add the brandy.

Use mixture immediately or cover and re-warm just before use.

Place sponge on a plate and sprinkle with brandy, sherry or fruit juice. Using a scoop heated in very hot water, make ice-cream balls and pile onto the sponge. Pour warm sauce over the ice-cream and decorate with fresh fruit.

Serve immediately.

For larger numbers use sliced ice-cream (not scooped) and pour warm sauce over the sponge rather than the ice-cream so that it does not melt too quickly, or fill sponge with ice-cream earlier than required, and refreeze. Cut into pieces to serve with the hot sauce on the side in a jug.

Happy Christmas!

½ cup mixed fruit, chopped
¾ cup water
2 tbsp vinegar
½ tsp cinnamon
½ tsp mixed spice
¼ tsp ground cloves
½ cup sugar
2 tbsp butter
1 tbsp cornflour or vanilla custard powder
1 - 2 tbsp brandy, or ½ tsp brandy essence
1 unfilled trifle sponge
1 litre vanilla ice-cream
red cherries and green kiwifruit

Egg Nog Sauce

Helen Macfarlane

This recipe was always requested at Christmas by family and friends. It has American origins and is really delicious with hot puddings, berries or fruit salad.

Beat egg until foamy. Blend in butter, icing sugar, vanilla, nutmeg and brandy (or rum). Gently fold whipped cream into egg mixture.

Chill until serving time.

1 egg
¾ cup icing sugar
3 tbsp melted butter
1 tsp vanilla essence
¼ tsp grated nutmeg
2 tbsp brandy or rum
⅔ cup whipping cream, whipped

Vanille Kipferl

Luisa Egger

These shortbread biscuits are always a family favourite at Christmas time, it is one of dad's Austrian recipes that originally came from Oma. Instead of Christmas cake and mince pies, Austrians have a selection of small biscuits. Mum and I make these every Christmas, although I will admit that in my younger years I did more quality controlling than helping, it is now dad's job to test them.

Any nuts can be used; walnuts, hazelnuts or almonds, we usually use either walnuts or almonds. The original recipe doesn't use eggs, but adding an egg makes the dough easier to work with.

Place the first 6 ingredients in a large mixing bowl and mix until just combined. Tip onto a lightly floured bench and lightly knead until you have a smooth dough.

Shape the dough into several logs (approximately 1½cm round) and wrap in cling-film. Refrigerate for at least an hour.

Preheat oven to 175° C. Cut off small pieces of the dough, roll them into small sausages using your fingertips and then shape into crescents. Place the crescents onto a pre-prepared baking tray.

Bake on the middle rack for 12 - 15 minutes (depending on the size of the crescents) or until the edges begin to turn golden. Remove from oven and allow to cool slightly.

In a large, shallow container combine the castor sugar and vanilla sugar. While the kipferl are still warm, carefully coat in the sugar giving them a good dusting. Store in an airtight container, they will keep for several weeks (if they last that long!).

300g flour
250g butter, cut into small pieces
100g castor sugar
100g finely ground almonds
10g vanilla sugar
1 egg

castor sugar
vanilla sugar

Rum Truffles

Pauleen Wilkinson

I was 18 years old, when we married in March 1963. The only thing I had ever cooked in my life was a cake, Perfect Cake, from the *Edmonds Cookery Book*. I know I had quite a few disasters over those early years. But gradually I became more confident and followed recipes from the NZ Women's Weekly magazine. Much later, dinner parties would have me excited about tasting new recipes. As part of my small glory box, I had purchased a dainty, bone-china coffee set and found rum truffles became the perfect accompaniment. To this day, rum rruffles are still my two daughter and two grandsons' favourites.

In a large bowl, add crushed biscuits, sultanas, coconut and rum essence. Melt butter, icing sugar and cocoa, pour over biscuit mixture.

Roll into small balls and then roll in coconut and set in refrigerator.

18 crushed wine biscuits
2 cups sultanas
4 tbsp coconut
rum essence
8 oz butter
8 oz icing sugar
2 tbsp cocoa
diced walnuts (optional)

Avocado, Lime and Coconut Cheesecake

Philippa Whitehead

We have an avocado orchard, however if you had to purchase these ingredients you would probably have to take a small mortgage out first! I got this recipe off the internet, the introduction talked about avocado's being a guilt free ingredient as the creamy texture mimics cream cheese. It is dairy-free and gluten-free.

Base
140g ground almonds
¾ cup desiccated coconut
8 large medjool date (pitted)
salt, a good pinch
5 tbsp coconut oil, melted or soft

Filling
5 medium firm, ripe avocados
1 cup freshly squeezed lime juice
1 – 2 limes, grated zest
salt, good pinch
1 cup coconut cream or coconut yoghurt
2 tsp vanilla extract
1 cup maple syrup or ¾ cup castor sugar
1 handful fresh mint leaves, chopped
2 tbsp gelatine powder
2 tbsp cold water
3 tbsp boiling water

Preheat oven to 160º C. To make the base; place all ingredients in a food processor and blitz until well combined. The mixture should hold when pinched together. Lightly grease and line with baking paper the base and sides of a 20cm round, spring-form tin. Tip in the base mixture and press down firmly and evenly with the back of a spoon. Bake for 10 – 15 minutes until browned, then set aside to cool completely in the fridge.

Place all the ingredients other than the gelatine and water in a food processor and blend until the mixture is smooth. Taste the mixture and add more maple syrup, lime juice, zest or vanilla if required.

Mix the gelatine powder with cold water and leave to swell for a few minutes. Add the boiling water and mix well to completely dissolve the gelatine (make sure there are no lumps). Add dissolved gelatine mixture to the food processor and blend with the avocado mixture until smooth and well incorporated.

Remove cake tin from the fridge and pour the filling over the base. Cover with a plate or cling film and return to the fridge to set for at least 4 – 5 hours or overnight.

To serve, carefully run a knife between the tin and the cake to loosen, then push the base of the tin up and carefully transfer to a serving plate. Serve with fresh berries or a berry coulis.

Right: Te Karaka Bay, Lake Rotoiti

Kessel's Butter Chicken

John Kessels

My wife Helen found a recipe some time ago and since then I have played around with it and have come up with something that my son and I especially like. We would make it at least 2 – 3 times a month before he left home for University. Now each time he comes home, I have to cook this recipe.

It is a very easy recipe to prepare and very easy to change the spices around to your desired taste—Lol go easy with the chilli!

600 – 650g boneless chicken breasts
diced into 2cm sized pieces
1 tsp crushed garlic
1 tbsp brown sugar
1 tsp salt
½ tsp ground black pepper
1½ tsp turmeric powder
1½ tsp cumin powder
½ tsp curry powder
1 tsp ground coriander
½ tsp chilli powder, optional
50g butter
1 small onion, chopped
3 tbsp tomato paste
3 tbsp tomato sauce—optional, but I like it!
½ tsp garam masala
1 cup cream
(or add another cup of coconut cream)
1 cup coconut cream

Place chicken into a large mixing bowl. Add garlic, brown sugar, salt and pepper, and all spices except garam masala. Toss together ensuring the chicken is well coated. If you have time, refrigerate for about half an hour to let spices flavour the meat. Melt the butter in a non-stick saucepan at high heat, add the onion and cook until soft, approximately 1 minute. Add the chicken, stir frequently until golden.

Turn down to medium heat and add tomato paste, tomato sauce and garam masala, stir in. Now add the cream and coconut cream and simmer with lid on the saucepan for 5 - 8 minutes, stirring occasionally until rich and creamy. Taste test and add more salt if you like.

Serve on rice (or mash potato if you want).

Butter Chicken

Adrienne Whitewood
Rotorua Fashion Designer

One of my nans quick and easy recipes was butter chicken. It's funny how when growing up the smell of 'boil up' came from most kitchens, while the smell of spices lingered in ours.

Make marinade by combining garam masala, coriander stalks, bay leaf, chilli, turmeric, salt, pepper and oil. Cut chicken into pieces and place in the marinade, cover the meat well, leave for a few hours.

On a medium heat fry chicken until nearly cooked, add the tomato paste. Take off heat, add cream and then simmer until cooked.

Serve with rice and poppadum's (optional). Garnish with fresh coriander leaves.

300g chicken breast or boneless thighs
3 tbsp oil
1 bay leaf
pinch of chilli powder
bunch of coriander stalks
1½ tbsp garam masala
1½ tbsp turmeric
salt and pepper
2 tbsp tomato paste
100ml cream

Chicken Something

Dame Susan Elizabeth Anne Devoy DNZM CBE
Former World Squash Champion and Race Relations Commissioner

Cooking is not my strong point, but this chicken dish, eaten as either a hearty soup or stew is delicious, and is even tastier the next day if there is anything left. It is the perfect comfort food.

Heat two tablespoons of olive oil in large saucepan. Add crushed garlic and cook for a couple of minutes. Add thinly sliced leeks and cook until soft. Add chicken thighs and some extra oil and brown on both sides. Add the pumpkin, tomatoes, chickpeas, water and chicken stock. Season with plenty of salt and pepper.

Bring to boil then simmer for 30 - 40 minutes or until chicken is tender and falling off the bone.

You can add some greens here either broccoli florets or peas or beans.

Serve with crusty bread.

2 tbsp olive oil
3 cloves garlic
1 leek
8 chicken thighs
2 cups diced pumpkin
1 tin tomatoes
1 tin chickpeas
1 cup water
1 cup chicken stock
salt and pepper

Aunty Bea's Curried Chicken

Beatrice Piatarihi Tui Yates (aka Aunty Bea)
Ngati Pikiao, with Scottish, Irish and Fijian Indian ancestry

Aunty Bea was a well known personality in Rotorua and loved by all. Aunty Bea has passed away since the original publication of this book but such is her legacy in Rotorua, that it was felt that this recipe of hers should be included. Aunty Bea was a teacher, author, an entertainer and was also involved in many charities including the setting up of the Te Whakapono Health Trust which helped fund the dialysis unit at Rotorua Hospital. The Trust sold the original *Volcanic Kitchens* book as a community fundraiser.

Heat the oil in a frying pan and cook the onion, garlic and ginger until a light brown. Add the chicken and gently fry for 10 minutes. Add the curry powder, salt to taste, paprika, turmeric, garam masala, tomatoes and water. Keep stirring to prevent sticking. Add the potato and mint.

Slowly simmer until the chicken is tender and potatoes cooked.

Serve with rice.

1 tbsp olive oil
1 onion, sliced
8 cloves garlic, crushed
fresh ginger, pounded
3 kg chicken (can be chicken wings or boneless chicken cut into pieces)
2 tbsp curry powder
rock salt
1 tsp paprika
1 tsp turmeric
1 tsp garam masala
1 can whole tomatoes
½ cup water
6 large potatoes, peeled and cut into ¼'s
2 sprigs mint

Parmesan Crumbed Chicken

Jo-Anne La Grouw
Trustee of the Rotorua Energy Charitable Trust

Preheat oven to 200° C.

Place the chicken in a single layer in an oven dish. Spread the mayonnaise over the chicken. Place the bread, Parmesan cheese, garlic salt and parsley in a food processor and whizz to combine, spread over the chicken, pressing to make it stick to the mayonnaise.

Bake for 20 - 25 minutes, until the chicken is cooked through and the breadcrumbs are golden.

6 boneless, skinless chicken breasts
½ cup mayonnaise
4 slices toast bread (crusts removed)
1 tsp garlic salt
¼ cup grated Parmesan cheese
1 tbsp chopped parsley

Left: Mural art in the city. Top mural is of Aunty Bea

Persian Style Yoghurt Baked Fish

The ingredients in this recipe are enough for 3 – 4 serves. We suggest using a white fish; either deep sea cod or hapuka, and if you don't have lime you can substitute with lemon, but lime tastes better. The original recipe comes from northern Iran and although fish and yoghurt may seem an odd combination, it works really well, and the breadcrumb topping gives added texture.

600g fish fillets
knob of butter
1 shallot, finely diced
salt
freshly ground white pepper

Preheat oven to 170º C. Butter an oven-proof dish, just large enough to fit the fillets comfortably, and spread with the diced shallots. Cut fish fillets into portion sized pieces and season with salt and pepper. Arrange the fillets on top of the shallots.

Yoghurt Sauce
220g thick natural yoghurt
½ tsp cornflour
1 egg yolk
1 lime, juice and zest

Prepare the yoghurt sauce by mixing together all the ingredients. Spoon all the sauce over the fish.

Walnut and Breadcrumb Topping
50g butter
30g coarse white breadcrumbs
50g walnuts, coarsely chopped
¼ cup flat leaf parsley, chopped

To make the topping; melt the butter in a fry-pan and then add the rest of the ingredients. Generously cover the fish with a thick layer of the topping.

Bake for 20 – 25 minutes or until the fish is cooked through.

Grilled Fish Tacos

Budgie (aka Mark Woods) and Joanna Price

We do love variations of this and really rate the marinade for the fish—the fresher the better!!

1 tsp salt
1 tsp cumin seeds
1 tsp fennel seeds
2 cloves garlic
1 tsp chilli flakes
1 tbsp red wine vinegar
3 tbsp olive oil
800g white fish (snapper or gurnard)
1 avocado
limes for juice
1 tbsp white miso paste
⅓ cup mayonnaise
1 red onion
125g watercress
1 orange, for juice
½ tsp salt flakes
12 small soft tortillas

Combine salt with ¼ cup water in saucepan. Bring to boil and set aside to cool. In small frying pan toast cumin and fennel seeds for 30 seconds or so until fragrant, then grind in a mortar and pestle. In a bowl mix the ground seeds with the garlic, chilli flakes and vinegar, whisk in the oil and then add the saltwater.

Pour this marinade over the fish ensuring a good even coverage. Set aside.

Mash the avocado in a bowl with some lime juice then mix in the miso paste (use salt if you have no miso paste) and the mayonnaise. Dice the onion and cover in cold water for ten minutes and then drain it.

Chop the watercress and mix in the onion, orange juice, lime juice and some salt.

Grill fish on BBQ (charcoal is best!) until just cooked through. Heat tortillas and assemble the tacos!

Enjoy with a good beer. Pacifico is our favourite Mexican beer, or a NZ beer to suit is Croucher Pilsener.

Classic and Wooden Boat Parade

In early February each year the Classic and Wooden Boat Parade is held on Lake Rotoiti. The first parade was held in 1997 with 40 boats of many shapes and sizes, taking part. The parade started as an acknowledgement of the lakes' history as wooden boats have been an integral part of this lake since first discovered by Īhenga, the Maori explorer. The full name of the lake is Rotoiti-kite-a-Īhenga or in English, "The Small Lake Discovered by Īhenga". Māori used wooden waka to navigate and travel around the lake. In later years, visitors from out of town had holiday homes on the lake and the numerous boatsheds situated around the edges still house a variety of classic boats from years gone by.

The event starts by the reserve just south of Okere Falls, spectators assemble on the shores to watch as the boats sail and motor slowly past. The parade then does a tour of Okawa Bay before finishing at Wairau Bay for a picnic and games.

Alf's Smoked Trout

Alf Hoyle

There are many variations of this recipe and every angler will swear that his/hers is the best. This recipe was given to me 20 years ago by Barry Spry of the Rotorua Anglers Association. Since then I have fine-tuned it to suit our tastes and the finished article is highly acclaimed by mates in rest homes and widows and widowers in Rotorua. In fact, some of the widows have been so keen to chat that they become very heavy handed with the sherry and on more than one occasion, I have had to walk home.

Take a well prepared trout (head off, gutted and cleaned).
Split the trout, in smaller trout leave the bone in as this increases the flavour.
On a firm board rub in a generous amount of sea salt and then a similar amount of brown sugar.
Put in an oven dish skin side down and place in fridge for 48 hours.
Take out of fridge in the evening and place in an onion bag, tail down. I use hooks to hold the fish up in the bag.
Take outside and hang up on the cold side of the house. (I have a small drying room clipped on the side of the house), leave until dawn next morning but avoid hanging in a full moon as the fish will go off very quickly.

The fish are now nice and dry and ready for smoking.

I am not going to give a time as each smoke house is different, as are the wood chips used (I use tree sawdust).

Just a word of warning: if you are using a small smoker as sold in sports shops place a heavy piece of tinfoil in a tent shape between fish and lid, this stops those small pieces of burnt sawdust flipping up onto the fish.

Best eaten as a finger food with thinly cut buttered wholemeal bread, and a cold glass of sparkling wine. The skin makes an excellent snack for your cat or dog.

Chinese New Year

The Chinese New Year is the most important holiday of the year for Chinese with celebrations traditionally spanning 15 days from the date of the first full moon in a calendar year. Because it follows the lunar cycle, the New Year date changes annually. The end of the New Year celebrations is traditionally marked with a Lantern Festival. Each year the Chinese New Year is celebrated by the Rotorua community with a Chinese festival held at the Rotorua Night Market. A range of Chinese cuisine is enjoyed with dumplings, pork buns, rice cakes and fortune cookies, and a much anticipated dumpling eating competition. There are cultural performances and the celebrations finish with Chinese dragons. These are a symbol of China's culture and are believed to bring good luck to people, the dragons are believed to possess qualities that include great power, dignity, fertility, wisdom and auspiciousness.

Pork Stir-Fry with Cumin

In a bowl combine the pork, soy sauce and wine (or sherry), cornflour and cumin and gently stir until the meat is coated. Heat the oil in a wok. Shallow fry the meat in batches for 1 - 2 minutes until the outside is browned and crisp. Repeat the process with the remaining meat. Put to one side and keep warm.

Drain the oil from the wok and wipe clean. Heat the wok over a medium heat and add 2 tbsp of the drained vegetable oil. Add the garlic, ginger, snow peas, spinach, carrots, courgettes and chilli, season with salt. Fry until the vegetables are cooked but still crunchy, you may need a little stock or water to prevent the vegetables from burning.

Arrange vegetables on a large platter, top with the crispy pork and garnish with fresh coriander leaves. Serve with rice.

600g pork loin
cut into thin slices 2 - 3cm wide
3 tbsp light soy sauce
4 tbsp Chinese cooking wine or sherry
4 tbsp cornflour
2 tbsp ground cumin
2 cups vegetable oil
1 clove garlic, finely chopped
½ tbsp fresh ginger, grated
½ cup snow peas
1 cup baby spinach, chopped
½ cup carrots, thinly sliced
½ cup courgettes, sliced
1 chilli, deseeded and finely chopped
salt
½ cup fresh coriander leaves

Zhongyue

Zhongyue and her husband Zhenhai live on the shores of Lake Rotorua with their daughter Cynthia, her Kiwi/Dutch husband Joe, and their three children. Cynthia is an only child (from the Chinese one-child policy) and as she says "where I go, my parents go".

The family moved from Auckland to Rotorua some three years ago for a change of pace and lifestyle. In Rotorua they are involved in the local Chinese community. The three grandchildren are bilingual and in the holidays are able to travel between New Zealand and China with their grandparents, experiencing both cultures.

With Cynthia and her husband busy with their business, Zhongyue does most of the cooking for the family while Zhenhai looks after the grounds.

Zhongyue's Chinese Dumplings

Zhongyue

Zhongyue enjoys cooking and this dumpling recipe is one of her specialities. In the northern area of China that the family originate from, the dumplings are usually boiled and not steamed or fried. Boiled dumplings are also the most important dish for celebrating Chinese (Lunar) New Year. The shape of the dumpling symbolizes wealth and eating them will bring good luck. There are no measurements to follow for this dumpling recipe, Zhongyue makes them by feel, Zhenhai however is required to assist with rolling the dough for the wrappers, that part of the process needs to be done quickly so that the dough doesn't dry out.

Dough
flour
water

To make the dough. Knead together flour and water, kneading to smooth dough, leave to rest for 20 – 30 minutes.

Filling
minced pork
shrimp, finely chopped
spring onion, finely chopped
egg
oil
Chinese cooking wine
standard soy sauce
dark soy sauce
salt
sesame oil
raw ginger, grated or powdered ginger
oyster sauce
Chinese chives, optional
(can be purchased in a Chinese supermarket)

Heat a little oil in a wok and add beaten egg, stirring as it cooks (you want soft scrambled egg and the oil should not be too hot or the egg will then puff up).

Chop shrimps finely and set to one side. In a bowl add the minced pork, and then to one side; add the spring onions and sesame oil. Marinating the spring onion in the sesame oil for a few minutes takes away the raw onion taste.

Mix a little cooking oil into the mince. By doing this the mince is kept moist and the flavour of the pork is not overwhelmed by the soy sauce. Combine together; the mince, marinated spring onion, salt, Chinese cooking wine, soy sauce, dark soy sauce, ginger aand oyster sauce. Lastly add the shrimp, soft scrambled egg and chives (if using them).

Garlic vinegar
Raw garlic
Malt vinegar

Marinate raw garlic in a jar of malt vinegar for approximately 2 weeks. The garlic turns green in colour and the vinegar acquires a delicate spicy flavour.

To make the wrappers
Knead the dough again; it should be firm to make a thin wrapper, if it is too soft the dumpling won't keep a nice shape. Break a ball of dough off, dig a small hole in the centre then shape it to a large circle. Cut it so that you have one long log. Shape the log into approximately 3cm in diameter.

Cut the log into small portion-sized pieces, dust with a little flour and flatten with the palm of your hand. Roll from the centre out, turning the wrapper continuously as you roll. This will mean the finished disc will be tapered on the edge and thicker in the centre to hold the filling.

Cook a small portion of the filling to taste and adjust seasoning if required. Place a small spoonful of filling into the centre of the disc, fold in half and crimp the edge to make the crescent shape. If you have one, place the dumplings on a corrugated dumpling board, otherwise use a chopping board.

To cook the dumplings
Fill a large pot with water and bring to the boil and add the dumplings (cook in batches). Slightly move the dumplings in one direction to stop them sticking. Place pot lid on, this cooks the filling, and bring to the boil. When boiling, remove lid and add a cup of cold water, bring to the boil again. They should be floating on top, simmer for a couple more minutes and remove with a slatted spoon.

Dip in garlic vinegar to eat.

Slow Cooked Pork Belly

Cynthia Kouwenhoven

Slow cooked pork belly, yummy. This a popular dish at our home, the kids love it and we cook it often, at the end you can add vegetables i.e., potato or Chinese cabbage.

Wash the pork belly and cut into 2cm cubes. Put the pork belly into a pot of boiling water. When it comes to the boil again, remove the pork belly.

Tip out the water and heat the oil and add ginger, garlic, fragrant leaves and anise stars. Stir-fry, stirring a few times. Add the pork belly and stir until slightly yellow on both sides.

Add the rock sugar, dark soy sauce, cooking wine and salt. Stir-fry evenly so that each piece of meat is coated with sauce.

Add hot water, enough to cover all the ingredients, have on high heat until the water is boiling again. Place lid on pot and reduce to a low heat and simmer slowly for 40 minutes to 1 hour. Remove lid and turn up heat, stirring until the sauce has thickened and coats each piece of pork belly.

500g pork belly
cooking oil
piece of fresh ginger, sliced
garlic, finely chopped
rock sugar, a few prices
fragrant leaves, sliced
(known in English as bay leaf)
2 anise stars
dark soy sauce
cooking wine
salt

Tomato Soup

Dame Fiona Kidman DNZM OBE, NZ author

Long ago I worked in the Rotorua Public Library with a staff of amazing women. I struck up a strong friendship with the deputy librarian at the time, Barbara. Barbara had a pile of great recipes, and passed on several. For at least five decades I made her bottled tomato soup every year. Below is the original. Contemporary cooks may wince at the amount of sugar, but the quantities make about a dozen half-sized preserving jars, so it's not too concentrated. I have added to it over the years; a couple of crushed cloves of garlic are good, and instead of parsley—for a Mediterranean flick—I sometimes use rigani, a wonderful Greek style of oregano that grows wild in my garden.

5.5 kg tomatoes
(beefsteak are the best for this recipe)
7 onions
1 cup sugar
2 level tbsp celery salt
7 cloves
2 tsp pepper
2 tbsp salt
1 tbsp parsley
450g butter
8 tbsp flour

Quarter the tomatoes and add sliced onions, add sugar, celery salt, cloves, pepper, salt and parsley and boil for half an hour. Put through a mouli and strain. Melt the butter, carefully stir in the flour, add sieved pulp and boil for 5 minutes.

Bottle in sterilised preserving jars and seal at once.

HM Dressing

Fay Olphert

This comes from my mother-in-law Heather Mary Olphert and is long-lasting with a wide variety of uses. The paprika gives it its distinctive pink tinge. This recipe is a winner, it can be kept in fridge for at least 3 months and can be used with prawns, mango salad and of course as a salad dressing. A Moccona coffee jar is the ideal size to store the dressing in the fridge .

1 tin Highlander sweetened condensed milk
1 tsp salt
280 ml brown vinegar
280 ml salad oil (can use a little more if desired)
2 tsp dry mustard
2 tsp paprika
3 cloves garlic

Mix altogether well and store in fridge.

Right: Sunrise view to the coast, Hoko Road, Hamurana

Summer Tomato Tarts

Joanne Bryant

In either a food processor or by hand, combine the flour and cream cheese until crumbly. In a bowl mix the egg yolks, yoghurt, salt and pepper. Add this to the flour and pulse for around 10 seconds or less.

Turn out onto glad-wrap and form into a dough. Chill for an hour or overnight (can also be frozen). Roll out and line the small, well-greased tart tins.

Mix ricotta and basil together in a separate bowl. Cut the cherry tomatoes in half.

For each tart, fill with filling ingredients.

Bake at 190° - 200° C for 20 - 30 minutes.

Pastry – makes 36 small tarts
250g flour
125g cream cheese
2 egg yolks
2 tbsp yoghurt
1 tsp salt
pepper

Filling for each tart
½ tsp tomato pasta sauce (San Remo)
½ tsp ricotta and basil
½ cherry tomato
½ black olive
grind of black pepper

Self-Crusting Courgette and Feta Flan

1 cup flour
2 tsp baking powder
ground white pepper
pinch nutmeg
3 eggs
500g courgettes, grated and juice squeezed out
1 red capsicum, diced
1 spring onion, sliced
1 clove garlic, finely chopped
½ cup finely diced fresh mint leaves
1 chilli, finely chopped (optional)
200g coarsely crumbled feta

Preheat oven to 180° C.

Mix together the flour, baking powder, pepper, nutmeg and eggs to form a smooth batter. Add the remaining ingredients, apart from the feta, and mix well.

Carefully fold in feta, you want some of the feta crumbles to remain intact. Pour into a prepared, buttered quiche dish and bake until cooked, approximately 30 minutes.

Note: this recipe does not include added salt as the feta is already quite salty.

Llanelli Pie

Jane Eyon-Richards

My wonderful husband Nick emigrated with his family from Llanelli in Wales in the early 1970s. He has never managed to convince me that Welsh food is better than what we cook in New Zealand, apart from this recipe. I stumbled across it in a magazine one day not long after we had returned from a visit to Wales. He had never heard of it so I think the pie must have been developed by a homesick Welshman in New Zealand.

I make it every St David's Day—and a few other times during the year when I think he needs a treat! Very rich and very bad for one's cholesterol levels so I have adapted the original to make it seem a bit healthier!

100g butter
½ tsp salt
175g flour
2 egg yolks
water to mix
2 - 3 leeks
225 mls cream
50g grated tasty cheese
salt and freshly ground pepper to season

Rub the butter into the flour and salt. Bind with the egg yolks and make a stiff dough with water. Roll out and line a flan tin with the pastry then bake blind for 10 minutes at 160° C.

Slice the leeks and cook for 3 minutes in the microwave. Drain any liquid then add the cream and cheese and salt and pepper. Spoon into the pastry shell.

Bake for a further 30 minutes (or so depending on how hot your oven might cook) until liquid has set and the top is lightly brown.

A&P (Agriculture and Pastoral) shows are a tradition part of New Zealand rural life. Originally started over 100 years ago, it was a festive few days of competitio and fun, including animal husbandry, wood choppir equestrian events, livestock competitions, dance and live entertainment.

The Rotorua A&P Show is held every January, and is a fun-filled day where the urban and rural communities come together.

Tortas Fritas

Lia Martinez

I came to NZ in 2013 just to travel around and met a New Zealander, and have not been back home since then. I have now made New Zealand my home, and have been living in Rotorua for the last 5 years with my partner (the guilty one for me staying here). I chose this recipe because it's very popular and I don't know anybody who doesn't like them. Back home, I used to eat tortas fritas when it was raining, my parents would cook them. I also remember going camping with my friends and eating them.

This is a very popular traditional recipe that dates from the beginning of the colonization of Uruguay.

Formerly when the 'gauchos' herded cattle and travelled from one place to another, they brought with them flour and salt, the only ingredients they used to make 'tortas fritas'. They made the dough by adding water, which they fried using cow fat. They cooked them with the heat of a bonfire, where they used to sit around to drink 'mate', eat tortas fritas and tell stories. The gaucho is a national symbol in Uruguay, a skilled horseman. These days, it is a tradition to eat tortas fritas when it's raining. Generally you make them at home, but you can buy them in some dairies only when it's raining. You can eat them with 'dulce de leche' (similar to caramel) while you are drinking 'mate'. This is a modern version of this traditional recipe.

½ kg flour
1 tsp salt
1 tsp baking powder
1 cup warm milk
oil for frying

Mix the flour, salt, and baking powder in a bowl. Add milk gradually, stirring and then kneading gently as you go, until the mixture forms a smooth dough (add more flour if mixture becomes too wet).

Separate dough into pieces, shape each piece into a ball, and flatten each ball into a pancake about ½ cm thick. Poke a hole in the center of each with your finger.

Add enough oil in a small skillet, and heat until fat sizzles. Add the dough. Fry breads in batches until golden brown on both sides, turning them once. Drain the fried tortas on paper towels. Some people like to sprinkle them with sugar while still hot. Serve warm.

Right: Redwoods Forest, Whakarewarewa

Black Pudding, Pear and Fennel Tart

Carla Porter

I first heard this Jacob Brown recipe on National Radio in 2008. We really enjoy it and find it is enough for 4 adults as a main course.

Mix the onion, sour cream, mustard and olive oil in a bowl and set aside. Cook the potatoes in boiling water until tender. Drain and slice into thin rounds. Cook the bacon pieces under the grill until lightly coloured.

Remove the skin from the black pudding and cut into thin slices.

Roll the puff pastry into a rectangle 13cm x 36cm. Place on a baking sheet. Spread half the sour cream mix over the top of the pastry. Sprinkle with shaved fennel and lay the pudding, potato and pear slices on top. Season with salt and pepper.

Cover with remaining sour cream mix and bake at 180° C for 20 minutes or until the pasty is golden.

Serve with rocket leaves and drizzle with a little olive oil.

300g black pudding
1 small red onion, thinly sliced
4 tbsp sour cream
1 tbsp Dijon mustard
2 tbsp olive oil
2 pears, sliced (not too ripe)
150g bacon pieces
3 agria potatoes
300g puff pastry
1 small fennel bulb, thinly sliced
handful of wild rocket leaves
salt and pepper

Rotorua Vintage Machinery Live Day

Rotorua Vintage Machinery Live Day hosted by the Rotorua Vintage Tractor and Machinery Club, is held every summer at the top of Oturoa Road, Mamaku. Here visitors can see a wide variety of old farm machinery at work; ploughs, tractors, stationary engines, vintage cars and trucks. Enthusiasts both young and old, get to enjoy watching the tractor and horse drawn ploughs from a bygone era in action, harvesting hay and cultivating the soil.

Frog's Spit Roast Pig

Clem on behalf of the Le Lievre family

My Dad (known to all as Froggy), was a farmer all his life and this is my version of his role when he cooked one of his many spit roasts, one of which was for Ngongotaha Medical Centre on the lakefront one Christmas.

Preparation time 6 months plus cooking time 6 hours!

1 Boar
1 Sow
6 months milk washings and food scraps
2 dozen lion red, chilled, plus extra for garnishing
firewood
director's chair
salt and apple, to taste

Place boar and sow in large pen for up to 3 days or until combined. Do not agitate. Remove boar and put aside for re-use. Feed sow well with milk washings and food scraps. After farrowing and weaning discard sow and store with boar. Allow weaners to run around garden for few weeks enjoying life. Transfer to finishing pen once lawn has been aerated. Baste 1 - 2 times daily with remaining milk washings and food scraps. When the porkers have suitably proven (to around 30 times original size) select one and arrange slaughter. Dress and place on long pole. Score the skin, tie down limbs and secure carcass so it doesn't slip while cooking. Store in chiller (lasts up to a week) with lion red (serve first dozen immediately).

Arrange for the rising generation to transport porker, spit roaster, second serve of lion red, director's chair and firewood to suitable event. Assess the wind and place director's chair in supervisory position out of potential smoke and drafts. Open first bottle and advise rising generation how to set up pig on spit, how to light fire (preferably with accelerants) and how to go home and get the extension cord that has been forgotten. Continue to drink lion red regularly, offering advice whenever needed and every 10 - 15 minutes whether needed or not. When the last bottle is opened the pig is ready to serve. Fall asleep while appearing to listen appreciatively to all the thanks from the gathered crowd.

Lamb's Fry Terrine

Lin and Joof Schaeffers

This recipe came about when we first arrived in Hamurana, our new neighbour gave us some lambs fry and pork fat. Joof, always one for trying to use everything of anything, came up with the idea of making a terrine. However, the old-fashioned way he had learned at Hotel School was a very lengthy process. We do like to keep a terrine in the fridge as a hearty snack, so we came up with this very easy, and a bit cheeky, way of making one.

1 onion, minced
1 tbsp butter
4 cloves, crown only as stalks leave a bitter taste
1 tbsp chopped fresh thyme
700g lamb liver, finely chopped
1 small cup pork fat, chopped
1 tsp freshly ground black pepper
2 tsp salt
1 garlic clove, grated or about ½ tsp
4 roasted garlic cloves
1 tsp grated lemon zest
1 egg
1 tsp red wine vinegar
1 tsp cognac/brandy
1 small cup Panko breadcrumbs
1 tsp chilli, we use roasted chilli in oil
5 thinly sliced rashes of bacon

Heat oven to 170º C. Cook onion slowly in butter until translucent. Add clove crowns and thyme and cook a few minutes more. Let cool. Combine with the remaining ingredients, apart from the bacon. Cook a small piece to check seasoning and adjust if necessary.

Line a loaf tin (5 cups volume) lengthwise, with the thinly sliced bacon. Fill the tin with the mixture.

Press down firmly and fold the ends of the bacon rashers over the top. Cover with foil and place in a deep baking dish. Fill the baking dish with boiling water so that the water comes halfway up the sides of the tin. Bake until the internal temperature reaches 145º C to 155º C (45 – 75 minutes). Leave to cool for a few minutes.

Place something heavy on top of the terrine to weigh it down and place in the fridge.

Mamaku Drovers hut

Short Ribs with Coffee and Ginger

This recipe is finger-licking good. The ribs are cooked in two stages; first the ribs are poached in the oven in a coffee and molasses stock, then they are barbequed with a coffee and ginger glaze. So, the first part can be cooked the day before and then finished on the barbeque when required.

Preheat the oven to 120º C. Mix together coffee, molasses, golden syrup and water. Place the short ribs in a rectangular oven-proof dish with the meat facing down. Cover with the coffee mixture, add peppercorns and spring onions and cover tightly with tinfoil. Place in the oven for 2½ hours until the ribs are tender. Remove from the oven and allow to cool. Once cooled, remove the ribs, retaining the stock.

To make the beef and coffee stock for the glaze; place the saved stock together with the other ingredients in a pot and simmer for 10 minutes.

When nearly ready to serve, brush the ribs with the coffee and ginger glaze and grill on the barbeque to warm the meat through and caramelise the outside. Keep brushing the glaze on until ready; this only takes a few minutes. Serve with the remaining glaze on the side.

1.2 kg short ribs
1 piece of 4 ribs cut 15cm wide
2 cups espresso coffee
1 tbsp molasses
1 tbsp golden syrup
5 black peppercorns
600 ml water
2 spring onions

Coffee and Ginger Glaze
2 cups beef/coffee stock, strained
½ cup light soy sauce
2 tbsp honey
2 tbsp fresh ginger, finely grated
2 red chillies

Tors are volcanic rock formations and are a feature of the Mamaku Plateau

Rural postmen and women deliver mail to a variety of receptacles; letterboxes artfully crafted from an array of materials, mainly using repurposed, pre-loved items.

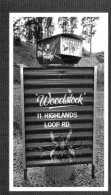

Rotorua Lakeside Concert

The Rotorua Lakeside Concert is an annual highlight event, a free outdoor musical concert held on the Lakefront reserve. The initial concert was held in 1997 in the pouring rain, it was the brain-child of local pharmacist Ian Edward, a singer himself. Set to appeal to a broad selection of the public from young to old, the entertainment includes Māori, classical and contemporary music. Families take along their rugs, picnics and the odd bottle of wine to enjoy an evening of entertainment. The fireworks display which marks the end of the evening is always outstanding. The concert also supports local charities and any donations received on the night go towards supporting the selected community group.

Timmie's Chorizo Risotto

Tim Beveridge
Singer, Promoter, Talkback host, Producer

This is one of the humorous and iconic recipes from the first edition of *Volcanic Kitchens*. Tim grew up in Rotorua and now lives in Auckland with his family. Tim has many strings to his bow, one of his accomplishments has been the production "The Music is Bond...James Bond", which he created, orchestrated and produced and which currently boasts millions of hits on YouTube, another has been his involment in the several of the Lakeside concerts, including the very first one in 1997.

Steep the saffron in a little boiled water and let sit.

"Soffritto"—or fry the chopped garlic and onion in 2 – 3 tbsp olive oil on a medium/slow heat until soft and clear. Strip a few branches of thyme to add to the onion and garlic while they are softening.

Add rice and toast it up a little with the soffritto for a minute or two. Glug in the white wine ttssshh! and reduce.

Add the stock all at once, don't fluff around with the little by little nonsense. Add chorizo at some stage, the earlier the better for the spiciness. Stick the lid on and leave on a low simmering heat.

Part way through, or early as you like, add saffron liquid. When stock is almost all absorbed, give it a good thrashing stir—'mantecare'—to release starches and make it creamy.

Season to taste if necessary. Stir in a handful of grated Parmesan a part of the thrashing, add peas as well.

Serve garnished with a little stripped thyme, Parmesan and cracked pepper.

DONE!

2 – 3 tbsp olive oil
(substitute with butter if you like)
2 cups of good quality risotto rice
1 litre chicken stock, heated
a few threads or a pinch of saffron
2 – 3 cloves garlic
1 onion, red if you like but doesn't really matter
a good glug of white wine
2 – 3 New Zealand made chorizo, chopped
(it is optional to fry beforehand to reduce fat content)
a cup or so of cooked peas, optional
fresh thyme, also optional but preferred
Parmesan cheese

Sneaky Treats for Dad and Daughter

Takurua Mutu

I call these sneaky because little miss was being a typical 3 year old and rebelling against anything that could be considered healthy. Smoothies are just an absolute winner for downing some sneaky veggies. Here's a healthy smoothie and a not so healthy one.

Healthy Berry Sneak Treat Smoothie
handful of Frozen Mixed Berries
1 banana
handful of baby spinach
½ mandarin
cup of water

Put in to a blender and blend….

Not so Healthy Banana Smoothie
2 bananas
dessertspoon of honey
2 dollops of natural yoghurt
2 scoops of ice-cream
cup of milk

Blend altogether, pour a cup for daughter.

With the remaining smoothie mixture add a double shot of espresso and blend again. Now you have your own, amazeballs, Banana Coffee Smoothie!

Chocolate-Lovers' Dream Smoothie Bowl

Rachel Grunwell

I was born, raised and educated in Rotorua. My journalist career began at the Daily Post and I am now a health, fitness and wellbeing practitioner and yoga tutor. In 2019 I published my first book, *Balance, Food, Health + Happiness*.

Avocado is the star ingredient in this decadent smoothie, which could be just as easily whipped up for dessert. I love avocados as they are delicious, but hey are also a 'real food'. The healthy fats in avocados are good skin-food and my kids love them as much as I do. You can make it in just a few minutes and then pop it in the fridge for a snack later. It's healthy and nutritious and I don't feel one bit guilty when I scoff it.

1 ripe avocado (skin off, stone removed)
1 frozen banana
½ cup of almond milk
3 fresh medjool dates (remove pips)
1 tbsp of cacao powder
1 tsp almond oil

Place all the ingredients in a blender and process to a smooth consistency with no flecks of avocado. Pour the mixture into two smoothie bowls and then "dig" it out with a spoon. You can save one bowl for later or give it to someone else in the house when you whip it up. Add a topping if you feel like being a fancy-pants.

For a protein boost, add 1 scoop of protein powder.

Right: Mountain biking is very popular, Crankworx is an international mountainbike festival held each year in Rotorua
Overleaf: Redwoods, Whakarewarewa Forest

Autumn

Apumoana Marae

Apumoana Marae is on Tarawera Road, Lynmore. The main hapū are Ngāti Kahu of Ngāti Whakaue, and Ngāti Tūmatawera and Ngāti Wahiao of Tūhourangi, all descendents of the Te Arawa waka. Their roto (lake) is Te Rotorua-nui-a-Kahumatamomoe or Lake Rotorua and the maunga (mountain) is Tarawera. The main wharenui or ancestral house is called Apumoana o te Ao Kōhatu and the wharekai (dining room) is Te Ao Wheoro.

Apumoana marae is very community focused, and with the help of local Bernard Hornfleck they established a large maara kai (community garden) in 2011. Here they have a large kūmara patch, an established fruit orchard and grow a wide variety of vegetables. Planting and harvesting are done according to the Māori Lunar calendar; October/November for planting, March/April for harvesting. The garden is not just for the marae—it is also for the wider community. Locals are invited to participate and grow their own food—the ethos is all about sharing the knowledge, providing food for the marae, minimising waste, self-sustainability and a community learning to work together.

The seed kūmara come from Dargaville and are then planted in the warm thermal area of Ōhinemutu until ready to be transplanted in the community gardens, of which there are several around the city.

Each week, some of the older children from the local Kindergarten 'Central Kids Elstree' have a morning on the marae with the Kaumātua Bob Te Aonui, during this time they help plant and tend the gardens, learn about composting and worm farming. At harvest time they take their kūmara harvest back to the kindergarten where it is cooked for all to enjoy, see recipes overleaf.

Chocolate Kūmara Pudding Surprise

Elstree Kindergarten

1 cup cooked kūmara
115g reduced fat (or non-fat) cream cheese
½ cup low-fat vanilla yoghurt
¼ cup brown sugar
½ cup chocolate syrup

Combine all ingredients in a blender or food processor. Blend until very smooth and creamy.

Makes 4 servings. Health food that doesn't taste like it!

Smashing Orange Poppa Bob Kūmara Smoothie

Elstree Kindergarten

1 cup cooked kūmara
3 cups orange juice
½ cup low-fat vanilla yoghurt
1 tbsp whipped cream
2 tsp vanilla extract
3 tsp low-calorie sugar substitute

Pour 2 cups of orange juice into a blender; reserve the rest. Add remaining ingredients and blend until smooth and frothy. Pour into a large pitcher; add the remaining juice and stir to combine.

Serve immediately. Makes 6 servings. Super!

Apumoana Kūmara Banana Pudding

Elstree Kindergarten

2 cups mashed cooked kūmara
1 cup mashed banana
⅓ cup of light brown sugar
¼ cup melted butter
½ cup milk
½ cup sour cream
1 tbsp grated orange rind
½ cup orange juice
¼ tsp salt
½ tsp mixed spice
2 eggs

In a large bowl, combine kūmara, bananas, sugar, butter, milk, sour cream, orange rind, orange juice, salt, mixed spice and egg yolks. Beat egg whites until stiff and fold into the kūmara mixture. Pour into a greased baking dish and bake at 175°C for 1¼ hours.

Serve with whipped cream if desired.

Mouth Watering Moerangi Kūmara Muffins

Elstree Kindergarten

Preheat oven to 180° C.

In a large bowl, combine kūmara, flour, baking powder, sugar, cinnamon and salt. Add eggs and oil. Blend/mix well. Fold in nuts and raisins. Pour batter into greased muffin cups until ¾ full. Bake for 15 minutes or until tops are springy.

Remove from pan and serve warm. Makes about 18 muffins. Yum!

1 cup cooked mashed kūmara
1½ cups flour
2¼ tsp baking powder
¾ tsp salt
1 cup sugar
⅔ tsp cinnamon
2 large eggs
¾ cup vegetable oil
½ cup walnuts or pecans
½ cup raisins

Red Lentil, Carrot and Kūmara Soup

Jenny Eaves

This is my most favourite winter warming soup. If there are any left over's, they freeze well.

Turn a slow cooker of at least 2 litre capacity to High.

Chop the onion fairly finely and put in frying pan with the oil or butter, the chopped garlic, and the next 4 seasonings. Cook a few minutes until the onion is transparent and the spices are fragrant.

While the mixture cooks, put the stock and the lentils into the slow cooker. Add the mixture from the frying pan, the finely chopped celery, and the grated or finely chopped carrot. Thinly peel the kūmara, cut in half lengthwise, and then cut each half in slices about 5 mm thick. Add to the slow cooker.

Cover and cook on High for 4 - 5 hours, or until everything is tender. (Do not expect chunky pieces of carrot to be very soft). Mash/puree until completely smooth, or blend with a hand blender.

Turn the slow cooker to low if you want to eat the soup later—within several hours. Just before serving, add your choice of cream, if you want a creamy flavour, and season with salt, pepper, and sugar to taste.

Garnish with one or more of the following; coriander leaves, parsley, paprika and small croutons. Refrigerate or freeze any leftovers.

1 large onion
2 - 3 tbsp olive oil or butter
1 - 2 cloves garlic
¼ - ½ tsp chilli powder
2 tsp ground cumin
1 tsp ground coriander
1 tsp turmeric powder
4 cups vegetable or chicken stock
1 cup red lentils
2 stalks celery
2 medium carrots
1 large golden kūmara
¼ - ½ cup evaporated milk, cream or coconut cream (I prefer the coconut)

Kūmara and Gorgonzola Gnocchi

Commercially produced gnocchi are usually smaller, however we like them slightly bigger in size so that you get more of the kūmara flavour and they have more of a bite.

Sauce
2 oranges
1 cup fresh cream
white pepper

Gnocchi
1.1 kg red kūmara
1 egg
1 egg yolk
pinch nutmeg
2 cups flour
salt
flour for dusting

Garnish
1 cup walnut pieces, toasted
50g Gorgonzola

Prepare the sauce. Squeeze the oranges into a small pot and reduce the juice over a medium heat. When almost evaporated, add the cream and white pepper, reduce again to about a ⅓.

To make the gnocchi; wash kūmara and prick the skins with fork. Sprinkle a baking tray with salt and place the kūmara on top. Bake in oven at 180° C for approximately 50 minutes or until soft (this will depend on the size of the kūmara). Remove from oven and allow to cool until you can touch them with your bare hands. Cut in half and with a spoon remove the flesh. If you have a potato ricer, push the kūmara flesh through. If not, use a potato masher to puree.

While the mixture is still warm, add the egg and egg yolk, nutmeg and flour, combine together. Tip onto a floured surface and lightly knead together until just combined into a soft dough. Be careful not to over knead, as this will give the gnocchi a rubbery texture.

Cut into pieces and roll into sausage shape, dusting with flour as required. Cut the sausages into smaller gnocchi, lightly roll them with your hands and dust with plenty of flour.

Bring a large pot of water to the boil and add salt. Cook gnocchi in batches, they are cooked when they float to the surface, about 3 - 4 minutes. Remove from boiling water with a slotted spoon.

Combine with the warm sauce and garnish with crumbled Gorgonzola, toasted walnuts.

Beetroot Salad with Polenta Croutons

This recipe includes pine nuts; however, you could substitute with toasted pumpkin seeds. Polenta is made from coarsely ground corn, and is also known as corn-grits; it is inexpensive and can be purchased from most supermarkets and bulk food stores.

Bring 1½ cups water to the boil and add salt. Slowly stir in the polenta, you want to avoid lumps from forming. Place lid on the pot and simmer for 5 - 7 minutes, stirring occasionally. When cooked, remove from heat and stir in Parmesan cheese.

Line a baking tray with cling-film and pour the polenta onto the tray, to approximately 1cm thickness. Place more cling-film on top and press down with a second baking tray so the mixture is nice and even. Cut into 1cm cubes and panfry in oil until golden in colour and crisp. Drain on a paper towel to remove any excess oil.

Place the whole beetroot, salt and cumin seeds in a pot and cover with cold water. Bring to the boil and gently simmer until cooked. Remove from heat and strain, allow to cool to room temperature. Peel the beetroot and cut into wedges.

Mix together the plum sauce and vinegar and then slowly add the oil, whisking continuously. Toss the beetroot in the dressing.

When ready to serve; line salad bowl with mesclun leaves, add beetroot and croutons and sprinkle with roasted pine nuts.

Polenta croutons
1½ cups water
salt
1 cup polenta
2 tbsp grated Parmesan cheese

600g small to medium beetroot
1 tsp cumin seeds
salt

Dressing
¼ cup plum sauce (see page 55)
2 tbsp balsamic vinegar
2 tbsp olive oil

mesclun lettuce
toasted pine nuts

Orange and Kūmara Salad

Peel and cut the kūmara into medium sized wedges, season with salt and pepper, drizzle with oil and roast in the oven until golden. While the kūmara are roasting, peel the oranges and fillet out the segments. Squeeze remaining orange flesh for juice and place to one side. When ready, remove the kūmara from the oven and pour the orange juice over while still hot.

To make the dressing; whisk all the ingredients together and stir until the honey is dissolved.

On the serving platter, arrange the orange fillets and kūmara wedges, coat with dressing and garnish with spring onion and chillies.

1 kg kūmara, peeled
2 tbsp oil
salt
white pepper
½ kg oranges
1 spring onion, finely sliced
3 mild red chillies,
de-seeded and finely diced
5 tbsp sunflower seeds, toasted

Lime and Honey Dressing
1 tbsp liquid honey
40 ml lime or lemon juice
50 ml good quality sunflower oil

Overleaf: Sunrise over the village of Ōhinemutu

Bev's Queen Sized Māori Bread

Pita Anaru
Ngāti Whakaue Kaumātua and a MNZM

The late Bev Anaru's life was dedicated to education. The Beverley Anarau Memorial Scholarships were established by her husband Pita for students who whakapapa to Te Arawa. Education apart, Bev Anaru was a dab hand at providing food for the proverbial 5000. In another tribute to his wife, Pita shares Bev's Queen Sized Māori Bread special in which yeast replaces the more traditional potato "starter bug". Use Edmunds Surebake yeast and canola spray to line camp oven.

Put 12 cups of flour in a large mixing bowl, add the sugar, salt and yeast. Add water and mix well. Place bowl in hot water to speed the rising of the mixture. Allow ½ to ¾ hours to rise.

When risen, add remaining 6 cups of flour and work into the mixture. Pour onto a floured covered bench and work the mixture thoroughly. Roll into two halves and place each in camp oven, alongside one another.

Put in hot water cupboard and allow to rise. Pre-heat oven to 150° C. Cover camp oven with tin foil and lid. Cook for one hour.

18 cups flour
6 dsp sugar
2 tsp salt
4 - 5 tbsp yeast
6 - 8 cups warm water

Left: The Galilee Chapel window of St Faith's Anglican Church
Below: St Faith's Anglican Church, Ōhinemutu

Women's Health League

The Women's Health League was founded in the Rotorua district in 1937, by district nurse Ruby Cameron (also known affectionately as Kamerana), and with the support of Te Arawa elders.

The league's focus was the health of Māori women and children, and it worked through marae-based women's committees. By the late 1940s it had spread beyond the central North Island, and its work on housing, marae support, ambulance staffing and alcohol abuse was having a positive effect on Māori health.

There are now six branches of the league in the Rotorua area.

In 2016 the Rotorua Branch, originally formed in 1954, was revived and has been taking part in the Rotorua Lakes Council Farmers Market initiative since its inception in 2017. Members use Te Ao Marama at Ōhinemutu once a month to make jams and pickles for sale, along with a tonic based on kawakawa— their catch-cry is "Pā Made". The main kaupapa is to use produce supplied by Sue White of Rotorua Fruit Harvest. The fruit comes from trees laden with fruit that would otherwise have gone to waste. The proceeds are then used to help finance outings, and social events for the Kaumātua (elders).

Ōhinemutu, on the shores of Lake Rotorua, is the home of Ngāti Whakaue, a sub-tribe of Te Arawa

Bottom Centre: Laurie, Ena, Ann, Leslie, Jody, Huhuna

Tomato Relish

Rotorua Women's Health League

1 kg tomatoes
250g onions, chopped finely
500g apples, diced
120g sultanas
750g sugar
1 tbsp whole cloves
1 tbsp salt
½ tsp cayenne—to taste—be cautious!

Cover with vinegar and boil until dark red in colour, stirring often, then ladle into sterilised jars and cover with sterilised lids.

Kamo Kamo Chutney

Rotorua Women's Health League

3 kg kamo kamo (courgette)
1 kg onions
1 cup cooking salt
water
1 litre dark malt vinegar
5 tbsp plain flour
1½ level tbsp curry powder
1 tbsp turmeric
1 tbsp dried mustard
1 kg brown sugar
2 finely chopped red chillies
(to suit taste)
1 finely chopped red capsicum
(with seeds removed)

Cut up the kamo kamo and onions, add the salt, then cover with cold water. Next day drain off almost all the excess water, test that it is not too salty, and then boil the vegetable and onion mixture for 15 minutes.

In a (second) large pot, mix together the plain flour (mixed to a paste with a little of the vinegar first), then the rest of the vinegar, curry powder, turmeric and mustard. Bring to the boil, stirring. Add brown sugar and stir to dissolve.

Add the cooked vegetable, red chillies, capsicum and onions to the vinegar mixture and bring back to the boil.

Cook for an further 10 minutes, stirring constantly and until you have the until desired consistency. Pour into sterilised jars.

Plum Jam

Rotorua Women's Health League

Expeditions to pick plums give us an old favourite jam, which can be made even nicer by replacing some of the plums with raspberries or strawberries.

Put plums and water into a preserving pan, boil until soft and pulpy. Stir often. When cool, carefully remove all the stones. Bring to the boiling stirring constantly. Add sugar and lemon juice, and bring to a rolling boil (over 200 degrees).

Test to see if it's ready by placing a spoonful on a saucer and placing it in the fridge for a few moments.

If a film forms on the top it's ready to bottle in sterilised jars and lids.

1 kg of plums
(Billington's Early or Black Doris are favourites)
375 mls (1½ cups of water)
1 cup of white sugar for every cup of pulp
juice of a lemon

Kawakawa Tonic

Rotorua Women's Health League

The kawakawa shrub grows well in New Zealand soils and the bark, leaves and fruit all have medicinal properties which are still widely used by Māori today. Laurie Morrison is in charge of making the kawakawa tonic which has good anti-inflammatory health properties. Bottles of the tonic sell well at the Sunday market.

The leaves are handpicked, the most nutritional leaves are those which are at the top of the plant and which the bugs have already nibbled at (they have holes in them).

Boil together and strain.

fresh turmeric
fresh ginger
saffron threads
cayenne pepper
manuka honey

Te Ao Marama and St Faith's Church, Ōhinemutu

Courgette Pickle

Our neighbour Rebecca occasionally arrives with home-made treats. This recipe is based on a jar of courgette pickle that she gave us one year, we took it to have with lunch at the beach and friends and family raved about it. A lovely pickle that goes well with cheese and crackers. Thanks Bec's!

Wash the courgettes and using a sharp vegetable peeler, slice lengthwise into long ribbons. Place courgette ribbons and sliced onion in a large bowl, add salt and mix well. Cover with cold water. Leave to soak for 1 hour, strain off the liquid and squeeze out any remaining juice.

In a saucepan, bring to the boil the rest of the ingredients. Add the courgette/onion mixture, bring back to the boil and simmer uncovered for 2 minutes.

Bottle in sterilised jars.

1 kg courgettes
1 medium red onion, thinly sliced
¼ cup salt
2 cups apple cider vinegar
1 cup white sugar
1 tsp mustard seeds
1 tsp dill seeds
1 tsp turmeric
1 tsp English mustard powder

Austrian Cucumber Salad

Jenny Lux

My father Heinrich Lux started Lewishams Restaurant in what is now "Eat Street" in the early 1980s, and he soon after founded The Steakhouse as well. Both restaurants had cucumber salad on the menu. This recipe is from an old Viennese cookbook of my mother's, Juliet Lux (nee Power), the daughter of sheep farmers Bob and Joan Power from Dalbeth Road. Juliet met Heini in Vienna, and we two children (Jenny and Kevin Lux) were born over there before moving back to Rotorua as a young family. I named my company Lux Organics partly because I like my surname and its links to my Austrian roots, but also because my Dad was well-known in food circles in Rotorua, having been in the restaurant business for over 20 years.

Peel and finely slice the cucumbers and sprinkle with salt. Leave to drain off water in colander, and then squeeze gently by hand.

To make the dressing, combine all the ingredients.

Add dressing to the cucumber, toss together well and sprinkle with sweet paprika.

3 large cucumbers, peeled and finely sliced
¾ tsp salt sprinkled over the top
sweet paprika

Dressing:
1 clove garlic crushed
1 tbsp olive oil
¼ cup wine vinegar
2 tsp sugar
pepper

Rotorua Marathon

The Rotorua Marathon first started as an official event in 1965 with just 16 runners; it is now Australasia's oldest major marathon event. Held on the first Saturday in May, it has developed into a huge event with thousands of participants. Coming from all over the world, with many dressed in costume, they take part in what is affectionately known as the 'People's Marathon'. The event has grown over the decades to include walking, half and quarter marathons as well as a fun run. The race starts and finishes in the Government Gardens and there is always an enthusiastic spectator crowd to be had, enjoying the occasion by exuberantly supporting the participants.

Cranola Bars

These are quick to make as they are not baked, the result is a chewy bar high in carbohydrates and with the added protein of peanut butter, they will provide the energy to get you through the day.

In a medium sized pot over a low heat, melt together the peanut butter, honey and coconut oil, stirring until smooth. Remove from the heat and add the rolled oats, coconut, cranberries, goji berries and almonds.

Pour the mixture into a square baking tin, approximately 2½ - 3cm thick and press down firmly.

Refrigerate for 2 hours or until the mixture has set. Slice into bars and store in an airtight container.

½ cup peanut butter
½ cup honey
½ cup coconut oil
2 cups rolled oats, toasted
1 cup shredded coconut
1 cup dried cranberries
½ cup goji berries
½ cup toasted almonds, coarsely chopped

Bubble Snack Bar

Luisa Egger

In a medium sized pot, melt the butter and then add the sugar and honey and mix until smooth. Add rice bubbles, toasted pumpkin seeds and chia seeds and stir to combine.

Pour into a pre-prepared tray covered in baking paper and leave to set, you can put it in the fridge to cool more quickly. Cut into slices.

100g butter
80g sugar
2 tbsp honey
4 cups rice bubbles
pumpkin seeds, toasted
chia seeds

Chestnut Soup

The autumn colours from the chestnut trees growing in the local parks are a reminder that the prickly fruit that fall in autumn have a tasty treasure hiding within. Roasting the chestnuts in a hot skillet makes them easier to peel and also enhances the delicious nutty flavour.

1 kg fresh chestnuts
50g butter
1 onion, medium sized
½ cup dry vermouth
3 cups of vegetable or chicken stock
1 cup cream
2 tbsp cornflour
salt
white pepper
pinch of ground nutmeg

Using a sharp knife, make a cut on the rounded side of each chestnut cutting all the way through the shell. Place them in a hot skillet and roast with a lid on until the skin peels back and the flesh inside is soft. Peel while still warm, removing both the shell and the inner skin. If difficult to peel, spoon the nut-flesh out instead. Separate some of the nicer chestnuts to be used for garnish.

Finely dice the onion and sauté in butter until translucent. Add vermouth, stock and roasted chestnuts. Bring to the boil and then puree. Add the cream and bring to a simmer. To thicken, add an equal amount of cold water to the cornflour and stir to a smooth paste. Whisk into the simmering soup, stirring continuously. Adjust seasoning with salt and white pepper and add a pinch of nutmeg.

Serve garnished with chopped chestnuts.

Butternut Soup

Luisa Egger

This winter-warming soup is perfect for those cold days when you just want to snuggle up in front of the fire with a good book. Also a healthy and filling dinner for cost-conscious university students, like myself!

3 onions, chopped
2 cloves garlic, chopped
1 kg butternut
5 small kūmara
2 small potatoes
2 cups vegetable stock
1 tsp thyme
1 tsp oregano
1 tsp mixed herbs
salt
pepper
sour cream

Sauté the onions and garlic in a large pot until golden. Peel and cut butternut, kūmara and potatoes into pieces and add to the pot. Pour over hot vegetable stock, add the herbs, salt and pepper to taste and then simmer gently until the vegetables are soft.

Allow to cool slightly and then blend with either a blending stick or in a food processor, until smooth. Serve in large bowls with a dollop of sour cream on top and crusty bread on the side.

Bobotie

Elize de Bruin

This recipe is a very popular South African recipe with its origin from the Cape Malay community.

2 slices of bread soaked in water (use gluten free bread for a gluten free option)
2 large onions, chopped
50 ml oil
knob of butter
1 kg mince
100 ml fruit chutney (or apricot jam for a gluten free option)
125 ml sultanas
125 ml flaked almonds (optional)
125 ml parsley (optional)
2 tsp salt
2 tsp crushed garlic (to taste)
1 tsp mixed spice
1 - 1½ tsp cardamom to taste
½ tsp whole pepper corns (optional)
15 ml mild curry
(check curry ingredients for gluten free option)
1 heaped tsp of turmeric
4 bay leaves
2 eggs
500 ml milk

Put bread in water to soak. Fry onions in oil and butter until transparent, add meat and fry another 5 minutes. Add all the other ingredients, except milk and eggs. Mix well. Spread into a baking dish and press bay leaves into meat. Bake at 180° C for 30 minutes.

Remove from oven. (Dish can be frozen at this stage after making sure that it has cooled down). Follow next step if not frozen, or after defrosting: mix eggs and milk together well. Pour over dish and bake again for 30 minutes until mixture is well set.

Serve with yellow rice and chutney on the side.

Chilli Fried Rice

Maureen Cresswell

I think this is a Julie Biuso recipe which must be at least 20 years old but I haven't been able to find it in any of her recipe books or website. Regardless, it's good for using leftover rice.

Heat the oil in a wok or frying pan over medium heat. Add the onion and chopped chilli, stir-fry for a few minutes

Add the curry paste and cook for a minute then add pork/chicken. Stir-fry for a further couple of minutes, until just cooked

Increase the heat of the wok/frying pan, add rice and mix well until coated with curry mixture and heated through

Beat the eggs with a fork, push rice to one side and pour in the beaten eggs. When the egg starts to set mix it through the rice and cook for another minute. Add the shrimps and peas. Sprinkle over the fish sauce. Mix well.

Garnish with coriander leaves and fresh sliced chilli.

oil for frying
1 onion, finely chopped
1 or 2 red or green chillies (depending on how much your family will tolerate)
1 tbsp red curry paste
70g diced pork, take the meat from a pork cutlet—or you may use chicken
1 - 2 cups cold cooked rice
2 eggs
70g cooked shrimps
2 - 3 tbsp fish sauce
¾ cup cooked peas
coriander leaves
fresh sliced chilli

Panhandle Hash

Gwen Ross

Serves 4 - 6. This dish has long been a firm favourite with my family, served with a salad or crusty bread. Nowadays, my two little great grandchildren are delighted when Granny makes it for them.

Heat dry frying pan to maximum temperature. Tip mince into the hot pan and cook, stirring constantly until the meat is browned. Add chopped onion and garlic. Continue to cook until the onions soften. Add salt, pepper, Worcestershire sauce, tomatoes, 2 tomato cans of hot water, sugar and basil.

Stir well and reduce heat. Sprinkle macaroni all over the surface of meat mixture. Cover the pan with lid and vent closed. Simmer for approximately 30 minutes, until the macaroni is tender, stir once or twice during cooking.

Prior to serving, sprinkle with plenty of chopped parsley.

500g beef mince (can be more)
3 cloves garlic
3 medium onions
3 tsp salt
generous sprinkling of freshly ground black pepper
1 - 2 x 400g can of chopped Italian tomatoes or tomato puree
dash of Worcestershire sauce
hot water
1 tbsp sugar
pinch dried basil (optional)
250g macaroni
chopped parsley

Left: Autumn colours, Centennial Park Maple Grove

Tasty Paella

Carla Porter

A true paella is cooked in a wide, shallow metal pan so that the rice is thinly spread and touching the bottom, when finished and ready to serve, the rice will have formed a rice crust, also called a socarrat.

6 tbsp olive oil
350g chicken meat, cubed
3 onions, finely diced
100g bacon, diced
2 capsicums, finely diced
3 cloves garlic, finely chopped
150g green beans
1 tsp paprika
250g medium grain or paella rice
salt and pepper
900 ml chicken stock
1 pinch saffron
75 ml white wine
400g raw prawns

Heat 2 tbsp oil, add chicken and stir-fry for 3 minutes, remove from the pan. Add the remaining oil and fry the onions and bacon (I sometimes also add chorizo) for approximately 4 minutes. Add the capsicums and continue to fry a few more minutes.

Reduce the heat, continue to cook for a further 10 minutes, stirring occasionally. Add the garlic, beans and paprika, cook another 5 minutes.

Add rice and stir coating the rice with oil and vegetables, season with salt and pepper.

Have the heated chicken stock and saffron simmering on the side. Pour the stock and wine over the rice and bring to the boil, reduce the heat and allow the pan to simmer for at least 10 minutes. DO NOT STIR. Add the chicken pieces and arrange the prawns.

Cover tightly with tinfoil and leave for at least 10 minutes.

Chicken Casserole

Barbara Cumming

500g chicken breasts
black pepper
3 tbsp oil or butter
280g fresh broccoli (or asparagus)
425g can of cream of chicken soup
½ cup mayonnaise
1 tbsp curry powder
1 tsp lemon juice
1 cup tasty cheese, grated

Sprinkle chicken breasts with black pepper, then slowly sauté in oil/butter until white and opaque. About 6 minutes. Drain.

Cook broccoli (or asparagus) in a little water till just tender and crisp (3 - 4 minutes). Drain.

Grease a casserole dish. Place chicken and broccoli in bottom.

In a bowl mix a can of cream of chicken soup, mayonnaise, curry powder, lemon juice. Mix and pour over chicken and broccoli. Sprinkle tasty cheese over the top.

Bake uncovered at 190º C for 30 – 35 minutes.

Serve with rice or your choice of vegetables.

Top and centre right: Lake Rotorua   Bottom right: Lake Ōkareka

Venison with Buttery Pears and Red Wine Jus

Carla Porter

This recipe came from Cape Town in South Africa, the original recipe uses springbok.

4 x 200g pieces of venison loin or one whole piece
cracked pepper
butter
olive oil

Season the venison with cracked pepper and rub with butter. Heat oil in a frying pan and sear the venison on all sides. Place in a pre-heated hot oven for 2 - 3 minutes, venison should be very rare. Cover and keep warm.

Buttery grilled pears
25g butter
2 pears, peeled, halved and cored
sugar

Preheat grill to hot. In a small fry pan melt the butter over a moderate heat and add the halved pears, round side up. Sprinkle with enough sugar to cover the pears and cook for 1 minute, shaking the pan from time to time. Turn the pears over, sprinkle with a little more sugar and cook for 1 minute more. Transfer the pan to the hot grill and brown the pears until golden, about 2 minutes, keep warm.

Red wine jus
240 ml red wine
1 sprig fresh thyme
1½ tbsp port
620ml stock (venison or chicken)
15g butter

In a medium saucepan combine the red wine, thyme and port and bring to the boil, skim and then lower the heat and simmer uncovered until the liquid has reduced by two thirds. Remove the thyme, add the stock and bring back to the boil. Skim the top, lower the heat and continue to simmer uncovered until reduced by half, strain into a clean saucepan, stir in the butter and keep warm.

To serve, slice the venison, top with pear and spoon over the wine jus. Serve with red cabbage and potato mash.

Venison Roast in the Pot

Chris Prenner

This is one way of making good use of that stag after a successful hunt—a nice pot roast for a chilly autumn evening.

Use a piece of venison leg muscle (about 1kg of topside or rump).

Seal the meat in a hot pot with a little oil. Once the meat is browned, take it out and put some diced carrots, onions, parsnip and garlic cloves in the pot and fry for about 10 minutes. Now add some pitted green olives and an average handful of pine nuts, some lemon thyme leaves and stir it all in. Add a good dash of merlot, heat up the sauce and add the meat again. Put on stove top or in oven and simmer for about 30 minutes. Don't forget to put a lid on.

Take the meat out and let it rest (cover with tinfoil), it should be about medium. Finish the sauce in a food processor or blend with a bar mixer. If the sauce is too thick for your liking just add some stock or more merlot. To finish, blend in a good dollop of cold butter and freshly chopped lemon thyme. If you don't have access to prime venison, you can use shoulder meat, but it is advisable to simmer it until tender—about 2 hours.

To serve—the meat should be about medium. Best served with butter roasted parsnip and celeriac, and polenta, see recipes below. Don't forget to season the meat, vegetables and polenta—but you know that anyway!!

Butter Roasted Parsnip and Celeriac

Chris Prenner

Cut the parsnip and celeriac into cubes (10mm - 15mm), put in pan and slowly roast in butter. Once the vegetables are soft enough for your liking, add some crushed Juniper berries and a little Rewa Rewa honey. Bingo.

Polenta Cakes

Chris Prenner

Cook the polenta and spread out on an oven tray (use baking paper on tray), cool, and cut into shapes with cookie cutter or just a knife. Now fry the pieces crispy in some olive oil. When cooking the polenta you can add some chopped pistachio, pine nuts or favorite herbs to it. You could also drizzle some of that leftover butter from the vegetables over it when serving. The best would be if you cook and spread the polenta a day or several hours before you need it.

Chris is a keen hunter, fisherman and chef who kindly keeps the author's deep-freeze topped up with yummy venison. Thank you Chris!

Left: Rainbow, Paradise Valley

Pork Steak with Feijoa

Cut two chillies in half, remove the seeds and cut into small dices. Pan-fry the chillies and feijoas gently in butter, and squeeze over the lemon juice. Keep warm.

Season the meat with salt, pepper and ground coriander and pan-fry in oil until just cooked through. Remove the pork from the pan and leave to rest.

In the same pan, char the 4 lemon slices and add the remaining 4 whole chillies.

Serve the pork steaks on a bed of saffron rice, top with pan-fried feijoa's and garnish with charred lemon slices and whole chillies.

6 red chillies
400g feijoas, peel and diced
4 x 200g pork loin steak
salt
pepper
ground coriander
oil
1 lemon, use 4 slices for garnish and the rest for juice
knob butter

Pork Piccata

This is a classic Northern Italian dish and there are two variations; one is to coat the medallions as you would a schnitzel—flour, egg and then coat in a mix of Parmesan cheese and breadcrumbs. The other is the method we enjoy most which doesn't use breadcrumbs. Traditionally this would usually be served on a bed of spaghetti with fresh tomato sauce.

Season the pork with salt and pepper. Whisk together the eggs and Parmesan cheese. Coat the medallions in flour and then dip into the egg mixture, ensuring they are well coated.

Pan-fry in hot oil.

12 pork medallions
salt
white pepper
flour
2 eggs
1 cup grated Parmesan cheese
oil for frying

Overleaf: The three domes of Mt Tarawera tower over Lake Tarawera

Mount Tarawera

Māori, we identify, orientate, or ground ourselves with a "pepeha". A pepeha is a resonating statement of pride, of belonging, of origination, of identification, stating ones Maunga first, then our sacred waterways, lakes or oceans, the name of the Iwi or tribe and Chief that holds domain. For my people it is;

Ko Ruawāhia te maunga	Ruawāhia is our mountain
Ko Tarawera te moana	Tarawera our sacred waters
Ko Te Arawa te waka	Te Arawa is our Waka
Ko Ngāti Rangitihi te Iwi	Ngāti Rangitihi are my people
Ko Mokonuiarangi te tangata	Mokonuiarangi is our great Chief

Today, Ruawāhia is commonly referred to as Mt Tarawera. It is made up of three predominant peaks, or Domes in volcanology speak. Each of them (Wāhanga, Ruawāhia & Tarawera) asserting its own mana, but collectively forming the commonly referenced Mt Tarawera.

Ruawāhia is the central, and highest peak, hence our reference, "Ko Ruawāhia te maunga". It is a mountain of majesty, of mystique, of Mana. They are all descriptive adjectives of the Maunga, yet none of them on their own do it the justice of its foreboding physical landscape presence, the intrigue of its steeped history, "korero tukuiho" handed down through the generations, and spiritual connectivity and dominance it commands. It is a massif, a sacred mountain of reverence.

The reverence of it being an "urupā" a mountain upon which our dead were taken on their last journey and laid to rest, this being one of the acute aspects of the tapu, the sacredness and the privilege the maunga permeates, the romantic intrigue of the beautiful maiden mountain Wāhanga, being admired by Ruawāhia, Tarawera and Pūtauaki, through to the devastating destruction and loss of life on that fateful night 10th of June 1886, the Tarawera Eruption.

My people, Ngāti Rangitihi, we are the Kaitiaki, the Guardians of Ruawāhia/Mt Tarawera. Looked at through a western lens, we have legal title in the Land Court of the Maunga, and yet we do not say we "own the mountain", we are merely Caretakers or Guardians of this generation for future generations.

Ken Raureti
Ngāti Rangitihi

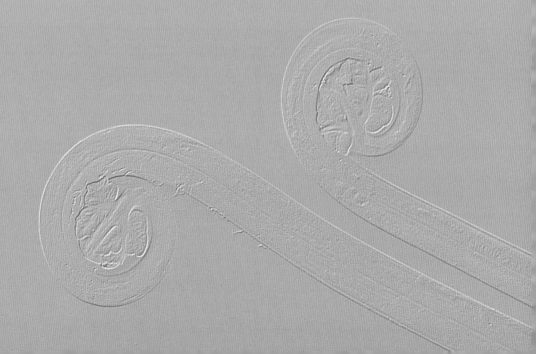

This sacred mountain of reverence (as referred to by Ken Raureti of Ngāti Rangitihi), sits along the southern edge of Lake Tarawera, the largest of the many lakes that surround the volcano known today as Mount Tarawera. The lake is peaceful, surrounded by regenerating native bush and a cluster of both permanent and holiday homes on the northern shore.

However all was not so. In the 1800's the lake was a busy tourist enterprise with local Tūhourangi Māori guiding visitors from around the world in boats across the lake, past the pā of Ngāti Rangitihi at Mourā Point, to visit the famous Pink and White Terraces of Lake Rotomahana. At the time the picturesque Lake Rotomahana, significantly smaller than the lake that is there today, showed signs of volcanic activity with many steam vents and geysers, and at one end, the famous silica terraces. These were the world's largest silica terraces, known as the 'eighth wonder of the world'.

That fateful night, June 10th 1886—saw the eruption of Mt Tarawera, changing forever the lives of the Māori living here as well as the environment and shape of the area. It started with a series of earthquakes, each one more violent than the one before—the earth was shaken. The sky was alight as the towering mountain was split apart, the peaks of Wāhanga, Ruawāhia and Tarawera erupted—spewing forth millions of tonnes of ash and debris and creating a 17km long fissure across the length of the mountain and through to the terraces and the Waimangu Valley. The Waimangu Valley was widened and filled with water, and the terraces lost under the waters of the newly formed, larger Lake Rotomahana that we see today.

Māori myth has it that in the days leading up to the eruption, well-known tourist guide Sophia Hinerangi saw a mysterious war canoe on the lake coming out of the lake mist. High priest Tūhoto Ariki of Tūhourangi interpreted this as a warning, the sighting of a waka wairua (a spirit canoe) prophesied death. The success of the tourism venture had had both a positive and negative effect on local Māori and the priest believed his people were being exploited and the ancestral values of the terraces and area ignored.

More than 120 people lost their lives, although the true numbers were never to be known. All of the Ngāti Rangitihi settlements and pā at the base of the mountain were destroyed with total loss of life. Many of the residents of the village of Te Wairoa, now known as 'The Buried Village', a local tourist attraction, survived—including Guide Sophia and priest Tūhoto Ariki, who was dug out of his whare some 4 days later.

Rescue parties came from Rotorua and Ōhinemutu, digging out survivors and providing shelter and supplies to the many homeless. The survivors dispersed, finding refuge with whānau at Whakarewarewa, Ngāpuna, Waitangi, Matatā, and the Coromandel. The government at the time took over the ownership of the land, which meant that the peoples of Ngāti Rangitihi were not able to return to the area when it recovered. The 17km rift which can be seen from kilometres away, is a constant reminder of the power the earth can generate.

Today, Ngāti Rangitihi are the Kaitiaki of Mt Tarawera, Ruawāhia is their mountain.

CAUTION
HOT WATER BURNS

Department of Conservation
Te Papa Atawhai

Fishing on Lake Tarawera

Fishermen (and women) come from around the world to fish in the lakes and streams surrounding Rotorua, and Lake Tarawera is one of the favourite spots to catch 'the big one'. The deep, cold water has an abundance of food and the trout can grow to an impressive size. The rainbow trout from this lake also provide brood stock for Fish & Game's hatchery breeding programme in Paradise Valley.

In late autumn, when the holiday makers have returned home, there is nothing quite like a quiet days fishing on the lake.

At the western end of the lake is Te Rata Bay, also known as Hot Water Beach. Here a hot water spring trickles into the cold lake water, with the thermal water creating a hot layer on top of the cold lake water. Steam rises from the shore and the sand can be extremely hot, up to 86° C. Perfect for cooking that freshly caught trout.

Te Rata Trout

An early morning trip with the boat out to Lake Tarawera, don't forget the chilly bin essentials; cold beer or bottle of wine (your choice), fresh lemons and lemon leaves from the garden, salt and white pepper, a generous portion of butter, some aluminium foil and a spade.

Spend the morning (or all day) relaxing with your fishing rod dangling over the side, listen to bird song and contemplate life while enjoying this very special and beautiful spot.

When you have landed a fat and tasty rainbow trout and your stomach is beginning to rumble, make your way over to the western shore and Te Rata Bay.

Clean your trout and fill the cavity with sliced lemon and some leaves, season well with salt and pepper and dollops of good kiwi butter, wrap well in foil. Find a spot near where the hot spring water enters the lake and using your spade, dig a hole in the sand until the hole is full of hot water, be careful as the sand is very hot.

Place the well wrapped trout in the water and leave to cook (as a guide, a good sized trout will take around 30 minutes), while you take the time to relax in the hot/cold water pool.

A perfect way to end a perfect day!

Bottled Trout

Alf Hoyle

I prefer trout from Lake Tikitapu (also known locally as Blue Lake) as they feed on koura and have a distinct flavor, but any trout will do.

2 trout about 1kg or larger
2 tbsp malt vinegar
1 tsp sea salt
1 tsp brown sugar

Fillet the trout and cut into small strips, leave small bones in but remove fins. Pack into jars quite firmly, and then add the rest of the ingredients (I use Quattro Italiano 25D. 8.5 oz. They are in packets of 4 and never fail to seal).

Clean around the lip of jars and tighten lids. Place in pot well covered, bring to the boil and boil for 4 hours. Remove and then, this is most important, tighten jars while still hot, the lids should pop within 5 minutes. Store in a cool place for 3 months.

To serve: open and pour off liquid, empty contents into a bowl and add a small amount of your favourite dressing.

Serve on dry biscuits. All the bones will have dissolved and are edible.

Tuatua or Large Pipis

Alf Hoyle

This is a beach recipe which you will not find in any recipe book until this one. It is so simple and the result is delicious. I had a cottage in the Far North at Cable Bay and the recipe was shown to me by Māori friends at Matai Bay.

1 bucket of tuatua or large pipis
A camp oven (small)
A tarpaulin
A blanket

Collect your shellfish and leave overnight in a cool place covered in salt water (they will expel all the sand from their shells). Next morning fill the camp oven with the shellfish mounding the top so that the lid fits tightly over and there is no room for movement. Boil a jug of fresh water, pour it over the shellfish, replace the lid and wait 5 minutes.

Boil the jug again. Pour off the first lot of water and add the second jug of boiling water. Quickly replace the lid and tie down tightly with rope, wrap up well in the rug and then wrap up the lot in the tarp.

Place in a cool place and leave for at least 6 hours. When ready unwrap and pour off the water. The shellfish will be closed and need a small knife to open. They have cooked in their own juice and taste like crayfish.

Thinly sliced whole meal bread, butter it and you have a meal fit for a king.

Right: Autumn colours at Lake Tarawera

Chilli Fish

Helen Macfarlane

Helen Macfarlane has done a bit of everything. She's been a military diplomat's wife, fashion designer, chef, interior decorator, tutor, now Helen Macfarlane's a published online author. For 18 years the Macfarlanes ran Poppy's Villa, Rotorua's first fine dining restaurant, its name saluted their favourite Bali eating place during their Indonesian years.

This is a favourite of Helen's family and harks back to their life in Indonesia where they experimented and soon became accustomed to adding chilli and other spices to their food enthusiastically, embracing the exotic cuisine of Asia after our seemingly blander cuisine of New Zealand at the time. Not so now!

Sauce
1 tbsp peanut oil
1 tbsp fresh ginger, grated
3 garlic cloves, crushed
½ cup chilli sauce
¾ cup tomato sauce
1 dstspn honey
2 tbsp soy sauce
1 tbsp dry sherry or ginger wine
3 tbsp water

Add ginger, garlic, tomato and chilli sauces to pan with oil and heat through. Stir for one minute then add remaining ingredients. Place in wok or large saucepan.

500g firm fish fillets
(I prefer to use lemon fish or monkfish)
1 cup plain flour
⅓ cup cornflour
1 large egg white
½ tsp 5 Spice powder (optional)
¾ cup water
oil to fry fish pieces

Slice fish into 2.5cm cubes. Sift flours into a bowl, add egg white, water and 5 Spice, beat to a smooth batter.

Dip fish pieces in batter and fry a few pieces at a time in hot oil for approximately 5 mins. Drain on paper towel and place in heated sauce in wok. Coat well with sauce and serve with boiled rice garnished with sliced spring onion tops.

Poisson Cru in Avocado

Helen Macfarlane

Serves 6. This dish was inspired when living in Singapore, though this is a French Polynesian recipe. Lime juice is my preference as is the zest as it marries so well with the fresh ginger and coconut cream, always tasting better the next day when the combined ingredients have blended and mellowed. Served in half an avocado.

500g terakihi or snapper
1 cup lime or lemon juice
reserved grated zest of 2 limes (lemons if used)
1 can coconut cream
1 red capsicum, finely sliced
1 spring onion, finely sliced
1 tbsp ginger root, finely grated
few drops of Tabasco sauce
3 avocados, large
1 fresh tomato, finely chopped

Slice fish finely into strips. Marinate in lime juice for 2 hours minimum or overnight until fish becomes opaque. Meanwhile combine all remaining ingredients except avocados. Drain fish, gently squeezing out liquid and save. Place in the prepared sauce and coat well. Change the quantities of capsicum and onion to your taste. Adjust flavours and add some of marinade if more acidic taste required. This is best if left overnight for flavours to mature.

To serve, halve avocados and place in individual dishes (slice a piece off bottom so they stay in place). Top with fish mixture. Garnish with spring onion curls if liked.

Seafood Lasagne

This recipe uses a creamy garlic cauliflower puree as an alternative to traditional white sauce. Use a firm white fish, we prefer to use ling if available.

Pre-heat oven to 180º C. Cut the cauliflower into rosettes and cook in cream with garlic and salt until just soft. Process in a food processor until smooth.

½ medium sized cauliflower
1½ cup cream
2 cloves garlic
salt

Cut the fish into pieces so that the fillets are all a similar thickness. Season with salt, pepper and lemon juice.

In an oven-proof serving dish approximately 20 x 30cm in size, layer the ingredients. Start with ½ a can of the chopped tomatoes, next a layer of pasta, ⅓ of the cauliflower, pasta, second third of cauliflower and then the fish. Next layer; pasta, remaining cauliflower, mussels, shrimps, pasta. Top with remaining tomatoes, basil, olives and then lastly the cheese.

Bake in the oven for 45 – 50 minutes until fish is cooked through.

500g firm white fish fillet
300g mussel meat,
(approximately 20 fresh mussels in the shell)
1 cup shrimps, shelled
½ lemon, juice
white pepper
200g dried lasagne sheets
2 x 400g can chopped tomatoes
½ cup fresh basil leaves, chopped
1 cup kalamata olives
2 cups grated mozzarella cheese

Lake Rotorua and Mokoia Island, Holdens Bay

Morello Cherry Cheesecake

700g jar of Morello cherries
200g vanilla wine biscuits
(or similar dry biscuit)
70g butter, melted
500g cream cheese
1 cup castor sugar
1 tsp vanilla extract
3 eggs
1 egg yolk
½ cup cream
3 tbsp cornflour

Preheat oven to 180° C.

Line a spring-form cake tin with baking paper. Drain cherries in a sieve while preparing rest of the mixture. In a food processor, pulse the biscuits until fine crumbs and then add the butter to combine. Press mixture firmly into the bottom of the lined cake tin. Place in the fridge until needed.

Cream together the cream cheese, sugar, vanilla extract, eggs, egg yolk and cream until light and creamy, then add 2 tbsp of cornflour.

Pour half the mixture onto the biscuit base. Carefully squeeze any remaining juice from the cherries and sprinkle with remaining cornflour. Spread half the cherries evenly over the cream cheese mixture. Pour over the second half of the mixture and smooth over. Arrange the remaining cherries on top.

Place cake tin on a baking tray and place in oven and cover with a piece of baking paper. Reduce oven temperature to 160° C and bake for approximately 60 - 70 minutes or until baked through. Leave to cool in the baking tin.

Lemon Yoghurt Cake

Elaine Fox

I don't remember where I got this recipe from, but it is very easy to make and in all the years I have been making it—I have never had a failure.

zest of 2 lemons
¾ cup olive oil
2 eggs
1 cup sugar
½ tsp salt
3 tsp lemon juice
1 cup natural yoghurt
(you can also use a citrus flavoured yoghurt)
2 cups self-raising flour

Preheat oven to 180° C.

In a bowl mix together the zest, oil, eggs and sugar with a fork. Add the remaining ingredients and mix until well combined. Pour the batter into a greased ring tin and bake for 30 minutes, put a skewer in to see if it cooked.

Remove cake from oven, allow to cool before turning onto a serving plate.

Decorate with lemon flavoured cream cheese icing.

Carrot Cake

Carey Bryant

I'm not a fussy cook, I prefer easy recipes with ingredients already in the pantry. I have a few favourite recipes, but I guess the best choice would be my carrot cake because it is requested time and time again. Once presented on a nice platter it has everyone saying WOW and then I am told over and over that it's the best carrot cake people have tasted, so I guess that's the accolade that matters.

The recipe came from a friend, Tasha, a very long time ago (when we were all having babies) and she would make this cake and invite 3 friends around for morning tea. We would each have some cake and then after we left, Tasha would eat the rest of the cake on her own!!! It's quick to whip up (especially when David grates the carrots for me) and is best made the day prior to eating to allow the flavour to develop.

2 cups flour
1½ tsp baking soda
2 tsp baking powder
4 eggs
2 cups sugar
1 cup oil
3 cups grated carrot
1 small tin crushed pineapple
2 tsp cinnamon
1 tsp salt
chopped walnuts if you have any

Mix all ingredients well and bake at 300° F for 60 minutes.

Icing
4oz cream cheese
½ lb icing sugar
1oz butter
1 tsp vanilla essence

Sprinkle the icing generously with chopped dried apricots, sunflower seeds and pumpkin seeds mixed together.

Below: Lake front, Rotorua

Chocolate Beetroot Cake

Suzy Brown

This is a favourite recipe, 'borrowed' from Jamie Oliver!

Preheat the oven to 180° C. Lightly grease the bottom and sides of a 20cm springform cake tin with olive oil. Cut out a circle of greaseproof paper, roughly the same size as the bottom of the tin and use it to line the base. Dust the sides of the tin lightly with flour, then tap the tin to get rid of any excess.

Break 200g of the chocolate into small pieces and add to a heat-proof bowl. Place the bowl on top of a small pan of simmering water over a medium heat, making sure the bottom of the bowl isn't touching the water, allow to melt, stirring occasionally. Once melted, use oven gloves to carefully remove from the heat and put to one side—beware of the steam when you lift the bowl.

Peel the beetroot and then cut into quarters. Push the beetroot through the coarse grater attachment on the food processor or use a normal grater, then tip into a large mixing bowl. Place the egg whites into a large clean mixing bowl and add the yolks to the beetroot. Stir the sugar, almonds, baking powder, cocoa powder and melted chocolate into the beetroot and mix together well. Whisk the egg whites until you have stiff peaks. Use a spatula to fold a quarter of the egg whites into the beetroot mixture to loosen, then once combined, fold in the rest but try not to over-mix.

Add the mixture to the prepared cake tin and spread out evenly using a spatula. Bake in the hot oven for around 50 minutes, or until risen and cooked through. To check if it's done, stick a cocktail stick or skewer into the middle of the sponge, remove it after 5 seconds and if it comes out clean the cake is cooked; if it's slightly sticky it needs a bit longer.

Allow the cake to cool slightly, then carefully turn it out onto a wire rack to cool completely. When you're ready to serve, melt the remaining chocolate (in the same way as above), then serve each slice with some yoghurt and a little drizzle of the melted chocolate.

olive oil
plain flour, for dusting
300g good-quality dark chocolate
(70% cocoa solids)
250g raw beetroot
4 large free-range eggs, separated
150g sugar
120g ground almonds
1 tsp baking powder
1 tbsp good-quality cocoa powder
natural or coconut yoghurt, to serve

Feijoa and Ginger Cake

Dr Neil Poskitt

Many years ago, we had dinner with friends at their place and this was the cake for dessert. We really like the combination of feijoa with the crystallised ginger. The topping with threaded coconut and brown sugar adds to the taste and look. It's a reliable recipe and is my annual 'go to' cake to take to work for my birthday. Also uses up some of our feijoas—we get lots at this time of the year.

1 cup feijoa pulp
1 cup finely sliced apple
¼ cup crystallised ginger, chopped
1 tsp baking soda
½ cup boiling water
125g butter
1 cup sugar
1 tsp vanilla essence
1 egg
1½ cups flour

Topping
50g melted butter
½ cup brown sugar
¼ cup ground ginger
2 tbsp milk
1 cup threaded coconut

Preheat oven to 180º C. Line the base and grease and flour the sides of a 20cm round cake tin.

Combine the feijoa, apple, ginger, baking soda and boiling water. Allow to cool. Cream the butter and sugar, then beat in egg and vanilla essence.

Sift the flour into the creamed mixture, fold to combine. Fold in the apple and feijoa mix. Pour into the cake tin and bake for 40 minutes or until cake is golden and just baked through.

While cake is baking, combine the topping ingredients.

When cake is baked, remove from oven and spread the topping over the cooked cake. Return to oven for a further 8 – 10 minutes until the coconut is golden.

Serve at room temperature with fresh cream.

Right: Kaituna River, Okere Falls Scenic Reserve   Overleaf: Puarenga Stream and walk, Waipa

Winter

Hinemoa and Tūtānekai

Over 300 years ago a beautiful young woman called Hinemoa resided on the shores of Ōwhata, domiciled by Ngāti Tuteamutu, a Hapu affiliate to the Iwi Ngāti Tūhourangi. She was well sought after by the young men of the Arawa Waka, for not only her beauty but her presence that exuded a strong character. Born into an iwi of Tuakana status and her father Umukaria, a high ranking Rangatira within Ngāti Tūhourangi, her role as a Puhi, meant her life was already mapped out by the iwi/hapū elders. In particular, as to whom she could marry. This for her was probably the issue that had the most impact on her strength of character that has become legendary throughout the world.

This story begins on the shores of Ōwhata where the tribes of the Arawa waka have gathered to compete in a competition of strength, speed, skill, agility, artistry and intelligence. To find the ultimate warrior so to speak. The day of the competition a young man of Ngāti Uenukukopako, an affiliate teina hapū/tribe at that time to Ngāti Tūhourangi, paddles from the Island of Mokoia with his elder brothers to compete in the competition. Upon reaching the shore the young men haul their waka onto the white beach sands of Ōwhata, "let the competition begin" they say. It wasn't too long into the competition when one of the youngest of the brothers begins to stand out. This was the young brother Tūtānekai. Athletic, skilful, intelligent, master of the kōauau and handsome. Where the young women of the tribe became drawn to him, he only had eyes for Hinemoa and she for him. But because of her tuakana status and her being the Puhi, he knew her parents and the iwi tribal leaders wouldn't consent to them becoming husband and wife, given his own status being from a teina tribe.

So they were left with only one option, that was to defy their tribal customs as secretively as possible. Hence they planned that in the dead of night, after the finish of the competition and all the visiting tribes had returned home, she would paddle across to Mokoia Island (the home of Whakaue-kaipapa, the father of Tūtānekai), guided by the sound of his koauau. However, her parents had knowledge of the young love, and so her father instructed that all the waka be hauled further on shore and tied down, making it impossible for a person on their own to move the waka to the water. In the dead of night Hinemoa makes her way to the anchored waka, upon discovering her parent's deeds, and her inability to move the waka, she sits on the rock Iriirikapua. There she ponders her dilemma while listening to the sound of the kōauau as it gently glides over the waters of Rotorua-nui-a-Kahumatamomoe piercing the night.

Overcome by frustration in her powerlessness to move the waka and the sounds of the kōauau, Hinemoa becomes enchantingly weary. Suddenly the sound of the kōauau stops! Stirring Hinemoa out of her weariness, inspiring her to say "I'm going to swim there." Therein she gathers her thoughts, (never having swum that far in her life let alone in the darkness of night) and gathers things that could help her in her swim. This being the takawai/calabashes that were netted together as a floatation aid. Then recounting the navigational skills learnt during the many wananga she attended e.g. the north wave swim into it, south wave swim with it, the west and east wave swim 45 degrees either way will take you to Mokoia.

She sets out on her swim to Mokoia Island motivated by her love for Tūtānekai, tirelessly swimming her one single focus was to reach Mokoia. Finally, upon reaching the shores Hinemoa makes her way to the hot pools of Waikimihia where she immerses herself into the warm waters soothing her cold weary body. After a while, warmed and relaxed she is suddenly disturbed by a male figure making his way in the darkness to the pool. Fearing the unknown she reacts unconsciously as a male asserting vocal authority, "who goes there" she says. The reply in squeamish fright "I'm Tiki, I'm here to fetch water for Tūtānekai." Hinemoa takes the opportunity to surprise Tūtānekai, and understanding his warrior mentality, she continues with her façade, "homai ngaa taha, give me those water containers" wherein she grabs them and smashes them on the rocks. Frightened, Tiki runs off to Tūtānekai to tell him, as Hinemoa had suspected, Tūtānekai immediately goes into warrior mode.

"Nawai tenei i tukino toku mana, ka patu, who is this person that dares to disrespect my place, I will strike him down" he says to Tiki. Hastily he runs to challenge this person who has disrespected him. Approaching Waikimihia and seeing this figure in the pool he calls out in powerful assertive voice "E tama! me whai waahi hei hoki ki te kainga tuuturu, Boy! prepare to return to your loved ones those whom have passed on to the world of your ancestors." However, he is totally surprised and his anger immediately subsides upon hearing the reply in a young loving woman's voice "E te tau! Ko aahau nei, It's me Hinemoa."

They lovingly embrace defying their tribal traditions and their elders. The rest is history, today that union is known as 'Te Hope o Tūtānekai or Nga Koromatua o Ngāti Whakaue.'

Paraone Pirika
Kaumātua
Born in Te Takere Nui o te waka o Te Arawa, Ōwhata, Rotorua, under the watchful eye of his ancestral houses Tūtānekai and Hinemoa.

The Rotorua love story of Hinemoa and Tūtānekai is well known throughout New Zealand and visitors can find numerous references throughout the city: the two main streets Tūtānekai and Hinemoa intersect in the centre of town; Hinemoa's Rock named Iriirikapua, where she is said to have sat looking across to Mokoia, is situated at Hinemoa's Point by the Ōwhata Marae and there are many carvings and murals around the city depicting scenes from the narrative.

The beautiful folksong Pokarekareana, originally written around the time of the First World War (arranged by P. H. Tomoana in 1917) has many versions, this is one about Hinemoa and Tūtānekai.

Maori	English
Pokarakare ana	They are stirred
Nga wai o Rotorua	The waters of Lake Rotorua
Whiti atu koe hine	Cross over to me girl
Marino ana e	For now they are calm
Chorus	
E hine e	Oh girl
Hoki mai ra	Return to me
Ka mate ahau	Or else I will die
I te aroha e	Because of my love for you
Tuhi tuhi taku reta	I have written my letter
Tuku atu taku ringi	I have sent you my ring
Kia kite tou iwi	So that your people can see
Raru raru ana e	That I am troubled
Chorus	
E hine e	Oh girl
Hoki mai ra	Return to me
Ka mate ahau	Or else I will die
I te aroha e	Because of my love for you

TUTANEKAI ST
1106 - 1155

HINEMOA ST
1168 - 1247

KIA!ORA

WAIKIMIHIA-HINEMOAS POOL

Ōwhata Marae

Ōwhata Marae is located at Hinemoa Point on the edge of Lake Rotorua. The primary hapū are
Ngāti Te Roro-o-te-rangi, Ngāti Hei, Ngāti Korouateka and Ngāti Tukutahi of Ngāti Whakaue, all descendants
of the Te Arawa waka.

The whare tipuna (ancestral house) is called Tūtānekai and the wharekai (dining room) Hinemoa; both named
after the ancestors Hinemoa and Tūtānekai.

Hospitality is an integral part of Maori culture. In this case, every second month, a meeting is held for the
Te Arawa Kaumātua (elders), where local politics, events and education are discussed. The meeting is followed by
a lunch served in the wharekai. Honor Vercoe and her team of helpers are in charge of cooking lunch: roast lamb;
roast vegetables; brisket and puha; pork and puha; fish frames and heads, and fry bread, finishing off with a
yummy dessert of apple and tamarillo sponge.

Right: Siobhan, Kathleen, Jo, Manuel, Honor, Rhyannon

Hot Apple and Tamarillo Sponge

Honor Vercoe
Ōwhata Marae

You can use any fruit for this sponge—apple, rhubarb, feijoa, kiwifruit, plum or a combination of fruits to your taste, or what is available at the time. End of winter, tamarillos are a little cheaper and if you are a tamarillo lover, this is a pudding to satisfy the taste buds, it is heavenly!

Heat oven to 180° C.

4 Green Apples
Peel, slice, wash, drain and cook with ¼ cup of water, if you need to add more water, add ¼ cup at a time.
Once cooked add ¼ cup of sugar.
Stir continuously for 1 - 2 minutes until sugar dissolved.
Transfer to small roast dish.

4 Tamarillos
Place tamarillos in a bowl and pour over enough boiling water to cover. Leave to soak for 1 - 2 minutes.
Use a knife to assist in removing the skins which will come away from the fruit quite easily.
Cut flesh into quarters, remove the hard core at tamarillo base.
Place cut tamarillos in pot, add 2 cups of water and bring to boil then reduce heat to simmer until pulp is cooked—darker in colour and broken down (if you need to add more water add ¼ cup at a time).
Now stir in ¼ cup of sugar, then keep adding ¼ cup of sugar at a time until the sweetness is at your desired level.
Transfer to same roast dish as the apple and lightly stir to combine.
Place in the oven—fan bake—180° C to keep hot.

Sponge
2 eggs
½ cup sugar
Beat for 10 - 15 minutes, the mixture should be doubled in size and pale yellow.

Sift together:
½ cup cornflour
1 tsp custard powder
1 tsp baking powder
1 tsp plain flour

Fold half the sifted ingredients into the egg mixture—preferably with a metal slotted spoon, until well combined.
Fold in remaining sifted ingredients.
Pour over hot fruit and bake at 180° C for 12 - 15 minutes.
Check before removing from oven by placing sharp pointed knife into centre.
If sponge mixture is on blade leave in for a couple of more minutes.

When cooked remove from oven.

Serve with custard and cream.

Brisket and Pūhā

Honor Vercoe
Ōwhata Marae

Pūhā is known to many as a common weed, but for many Māori it is a nutritional herb and often eaten as part of a 'boil-up'. Also known as sow thistle or milk thistle, pūhā is rich in vitamins A, B1, B2, Niacin, vitamin C and many minerals. The pūhā cooked on the Ōwhata Marae was gathered in Murupara. It can be bitter, so is best washed and bruised as this takes away some of the bitter taste.

Cut brisket into small bite-size pieces. Wash and place in pot. Add enough cold water to just cover the meat. Sprinkle a good amount of salt—depending on pot size, it could be 2 teaspoons or 2 dessertspoons. Bring to boil then turn down to a slow boil.

While meat is cooking for the next hour and a half, remember to check the water and have a quick taste if enough salt. Add a bit more if required.

Clean pūhā and wash three times. After the 3rd wash, take a handful of pūhā and with two hands rub and squeeze out the water. Break the pūhā by turning your hands in opposite directions.

Place pūhā on top of boiling meat. Continue in this way until all the pūhā is in the pot. Again check salt content and water level. Add more if necessary. Using a wooden spoon push the pūhā into and under the water.

Pūhā should be cooked in 20 to 30 minutes. Keep checking the water level and maintain it to just covering the meat and pūhā.

Fry Bread

Siobhan Petera
Ōwhata Marae

5 kg flour
2 litres warm water
little milk
little sugar to activate yeast
4 tbsp yeast

Mix the water, milk, sugar and yeast, put to one side for the yeast to activate. Tip the activated mixture into the flour, combine with your hands and knead to a firm dough. Leave in a warm place for the dough to rise.

Knead again, leave to rise—do this process three times.

Cut the dough into flat pieces and deep-fry in hot oil.

Venison Horopito Burger

Makes 4 man-sized burgers or 6 for those with a smaller appetite. Instead of a traditional burger bun try fry-bread, venison is a lean meat so the calories are counterbalanced, a little bit anyway! The advantage of this recipe is that it does not include eggs, this means a firmer patty which is easier to cook on the barbeque. The most important part is to keep the meat very cold, prior to mixing place the meat in the deep-freeze for 30 minutes, or until the outside starts to freeze.

Put all the ingredients in a mixing bowl and mix very well as you would a dough, either by hand or with a food mixer. Divide into 4 (or 6) equal portions and form the burger patty. Grill on a hot plate and serve on warm fry-bread with your choice of toppings.

We enjoy them topped with beetroot chutney.

600g venison mince
4 tbsp plum sauce
4 tbsp milk powder
2 tbsp Worcestershire sauce
salt
Horopito powder to taste

Snow on Mt Tarawera, Rotorua

Pork and Pāua Pies

Pāua is the Māori name for abalone and is iconic to New Zealand. The colourful shell is used in traditional and contemporary art and the richly flavoured meat is considered a delicacy. Pāua are found in the coastal waters around the country and have always been a food source for Māori; playing a significant role in manaakitanga. This recipe uses spinach but you could also use watercress or pūhā. Pūhā needs to be washed and bruised prior to cooking, see page 172 for instructions.

Sauté the onions and garlic in oil until translucent. Add the pork and pāua, sauté for another 4 - 5 minutes, add the lemon zest and seasonings.

Pour in the cream and slowly simmer for about an hour with the lid off, stirring frequently. Once most of the liquid has evaporated, increase the heat and add the coarsely chopped spinach leaves. Cook for another 2 - 3 minutes until the spinach has wilted, season to taste and leave to cool.

Preheat the oven to 220º C. Grease the pie tins and line with puff pastry, allowing an extra 1½ cm higher than the height of the pie tin. Fill with the cooled pāua mixture and fold down the sides. Brush the pastry with egg wash and place a pastry lid on top, pressing down firmly to seal and then pierce with a fork to allow the steam to escape. Brush with egg wash.

Place the pies in the oven and reduce the heat to 175º C, bake for 20 - 40 minutes, depending on this size of your pie tin.

2 medium sized onion, finely diced
2 cloves garlic, finely chopped
2 tbsp cooking oil
500g pāua, finely minced
500g pork, finely minced
1 lemon, zest
salt, pepper and nutmeg to taste
500 ml cream
½ bunch fresh spinach, pūhā or watercress
pre-rolled flaky puff pastry
1 egg, for egg wash

Mussel Fritters

You will often find mussel fritters sold at markets, a large fritter cooked on the barbeque and served on a slice of white bread with a squirt of tomato sauce—a real kiwi treat.

Place the mussels in a large pot with the lid on, and steam open. The mussels need to be just open rather than cooked through. Strain and reserve the liquid.

Remove the mussel from the shell, take off the tongue and coarsely dice the mussel meat, you can leave the tongue in, but it is quite tough.

Whisk the eggs and liquid together, add flour and baking powder—mixing to a smooth batter. Add the remaining ingredients, including the mussel meat; adjust the seasonings to your taste.

Heat a little oil in a frying pan and place on medium heat. Drop spoonfuls of batter into the hot oil and cook for around 2 – 3 minutes on each side or until cooked through. They should be golden and crisp.

Best served piping hot.

1 kg fresh green-lipped mussels, approximately 300g mussel meat
2 eggs
¼ cup liquid, either juice from steamed mussels or milk
½ cup plain flour
½ tsp baking powder
¼ cup onions, finely diced
¼ cup parsley, coarsely chopped
salt
ground white pepper
pinch of nutmeg
1 tsp mild curry powder
vegetable oil for frying

JUMBO MUSSEL FRITTER

NZ WHITE BAIT FRITTER

PAUA FRITTER

The Rotorua markets include a variety of street food, locally baked breads and cakes, fresh produce, great coffee and interesting selections of locally made gifts and jewellery—all to be enjoyed while listening to local music.

Thursday Night Market, Rotorua North Rotary Kuirau Park Saturday Market, Sunday Farmers Market.

Smoky Jo Soup

Sue Gunn

This hearty winter soup is rich and full of flavour, especially with the Chipotle chillies which add a lovely smokiness.
Serve with crusty sourdough bread.

1 ham or bacon hock
2 dried chipotle chillies or
1 tsp of Chipotle in Adobo Sauce
2 tbsp olive oil
2 onions, finely diced
2 cloves garlic, crushed
1 tsp fennel seeds, roughly crushed
1 tsp cumin seeds, roughly crushed
1 tsp smoked paprika
2 chorizo sausages, thinly sliced
2 x 400g cans of beans, such as cannellini
and red kidney beans (can do one of each)
drained and rinsed
400g can chopped tomatoes in juice
salt and pepper to taste

Simmer a ham or bacon hock long and slow for a couple of hours, adding more water as required. Then use this cooking liquid as a stock for the soup. Chipotle chillies add a lovely smokiness; however the soup is still excellent without them.

While ham is cooking, pour ½ cup boiling water over dried chipotle chillies if using, and leave to soak for 30 minutes.

Lift ham hock out of the liquid, reserve the liquid. Cool ham and cut into small chunks, discarding skin and fat.

Heat oil in large pot and gently cook onions with garlic, fennel seeds, cumin seeds and smoked paprika until softened but not browned (about 5 minutes). Add chorizo and chopped ham and cook another 1 - 2 minutes. If using chipotle chillies, lift out of liquid, chop, discarding seeds. Add to soup with their soaking liquid or add the 1 teaspoon of chipotle sauce to soup.

Add beans and tomatoes to the pot along with 4 cups of the cooking liquid from the ham hock. Cover and simmer for 30 minutes to develop flavours.

When ready to serve, adjust seasoning to taste.

Beetroot Soup

Suzy Brown

Beetroot and orange kūmara are two of my favourite vegetables. I use beautiful organic red and orange beets from Lux Organics.

1 onion, peeled and sliced
4 cloves garlic, peeled and chopped
knob of ginger, peeled and grated
2 large beetroot, peeled and chopped
2 carrots, peeled and chopped
1 litre vegetable stock
1 tin organic coconut cream
salt
pepper

Sweat onion, garlic and ginger until soft, add vegetables. Cook for 2 mins. Add vegetable stock, enough to cover, might need to top up during boiling. Cook until beetroot is soft. Blend with coconut cream until desired consistency. Season as required.

Garnish with chopped herbs and a swirl of coconut or dairy yoghurt.

Carrot and Red Lentil Dhal

Jackie Blue MNZM

Here is the recipe that my family and I just love. It is so healthy. My youngest daughter discovered it online and introduced us to it. I make it frequently and its fame has spread far and wide. I have even adapted it to make in a pressure cooker and it turns out just as good. Best served on naan or pita bread with some stir-fried vegetables.

Heat oil in a non-stick saucepan. Add seeds. Fry until mustard seeds start to pop. Add carrot and cook, stirring, for 10 minutes. Add stock, water and lentils and simmer for 30 minutes. Stir in peanut butter and curry powder. Season. Simmer until thickened.

Serve on naan or pita bread with low-fat yoghurt, stir-fried vegetables and garnish with fresh coriander leaves.

oil
1 tsp black mustard seeds
1 tsp cumin seeds
500g grated carrot
500 ml low-salt vegetable stock
500 ml water
½ cup split red lentils, washed
1 - 2 tbsp crunchy peanut butter
1 tbsp curry powder
low-fat natural yoghurt, to serve
fresh coriander leaves, to garnish
pita naan or bread, to serve

Southern Corn Chowder

Helen Macfarlane

Once again a favourite recipe from an American military wife and now one of my most requested recipes. Quick and easy to make and served with garlic bread, there is never a scrap left over in the pot or on the plate. Always tastes better the day after being made. Great Sunday night meal!

Melt butter in pot on stove and sauté onion and bacon until translucent. Add potatoes and chicken stock. Simmer until potatoes are semi-soft then add creamed corn and milk. Simmer further until potatoes are soft then add cream and season to taste. Heat through. Serve with garlic bread.

If liked, garnish with crisped bacon pieces and chopped parsley

25g butter
1 medium onion, finely chopped
2 rashers of bacon, chopped
1 large potato cut into small cubes
3 cups chicken stock
400g tin of creamed corn
½ cup milk
¾ cup cream
salt and pepper

Golden Baked Cauliflower

This an easy method of cooking cauliflower and can be eaten by itself as a light lunch or as a side dish with your main meal. The sumac is optional but gives an added zing to the spicy flavours.

Preheat oven to 170º C. Prepare the cauliflower by first removing the large outer leaves, cut the base so that it sits flat and then using a pointed, narrow bladed knife—remove the centre of the stem—take care to ensure the cauliflower remains in one piece. Place in a roasting tray.

Place the fennel seeds and chilli flakes in a mortar and using the pestle, crush them together. Put the oil into a small saucepan and add the crushed fennel/chilli, turmeric and sumac and bring up to a temperature of around 60º C.

Slowly pour the oil and spices over the cauliflower, gently rubbing into the florets. Sprinkle with rock salt, lightly cover with tin foil and bake in the oven for 40 – 45 minutes, depending on how crunchy you like your cauliflower.

1 medium sized cauliflower
2 tsp fennel seeds
½ tsp chilli flakes
1 tsp ground turmeric
½ tsp sumac (optional)
¼ cup olive oil
rock salt

Roasted Winter Vegetables with Hazelnuts

This is a great winter vegetable dish and the hazelnuts add a lovely crunch.

Preheat oven to 200º C. Remove the outer leaves from the brussel sprouts and cut a deep 'x' into the base of each stalk. Place the brussel sprouts, carrots and whole mushrooms in a roasting tray and drizzle with sunflower oil. Sprinkle over the sunflower seeds and season with salt.

Bake in the oven for around 15 minutes; add the hazelnuts and return to the oven for a further 5 minutes—or until the vegetables are cooked through, but still crunchy.

Remove from oven and sprinkle with coriander to serve.

600g brussel sprouts
200g baby carrot, scrubbed and cut lengthwise in half
200g portobello mushrooms
2 tbsp sunflower oil
1 tsp cumin seeds
salt
1 cup hazelnuts, halved
½ cup fresh coriander leaves, chopped

Sweet and Sour Chicken with Coconut Rice

Kelly Mihaka
Rotorua Journalist and Entertainer

As a journalist, working mother of three girls, pre-school twins included, and with regular singing engagements I lead a fairly hectic life but I'm super conscious of trying not to always eat on the run for convenience, especially when it comes to my children. I am also coeliac which makes life a little trickier when it comes to ensuring ingredients are gluten-free while still being tasty. This recipe is fast becoming one of our favourites because it's really easy and adaptable to make it appear like a different meal by simply swapping out a few ingredients, while always maintaining gluten-free ingredients.

We all love a good winter casserole, but sometimes they can all taste the same and if you slow cook for too long, your meat becomes dry and tasteless. This one is different and I promise you the kids will love it.

1 kg of skinless chicken thighs
1 tbsp cornflour
1 tsp of fresh ginger
1 tsp of fresh garlic
½ cup tomato sauce
¼ cup brown sugar
¼ cup apple cider vinegar
2 tbsp gluten free soy sauce
1 onion
2 - 3 vegetables of choice
(I usually use capsicum, carrots, parsnip, mushrooms, courgettes, frozen corn kernels, fresh spinach, broccoli)
2 cups jasmine rice
165ml can Trident premium coconut cream
1 tsp salt
2⅓ cup water

Spray a casserole dish with olive oil cooking spray. In the dish, dust the fresh chicken thighs with cornflour. In a separate bowl, mix together ginger, garlic, tomato sauce, sugar, apple cider vinegar and soy sauce. Pour over chicken. Add the onion and vegetables of your choice (if using spinach, frozen corn kernels and broccoli, leave those out until the last hour of cooking).

Mix everything together carefully, cover and cook in an oven at 160° C for 2 hours.

While it is cooking, in a large pot add together rice, coconut cream, salt and water. Stir well. Cover and bring to the boil (set your oven's timer for about 3 minutes so you don't over boil and it makes a mess all over your stovetop), stir thoroughly and replace lid, simmer on a low temperature for 7 minutes only (set your oven's timer again!), turn off after 7 minutes and leave on the element (do not open the lid or stir again). Leave to absorb and fluff with a fork about half an hour later.

Some other ideas to make it a bit different:
Have mashed potato or mashed kūmara instead of rice and swap out the chicken for diced pork. It's also nice with pork loin chops done in a slow cooker for 7 - 8 hours on low.

Gumbo

Christian Thurston
Minnesota Opera Resident Artist

I feel extremely privileged to have grown up in a place like Rotorua. When a town celebrates culture and heritage so much, it creates an amazing melting pot of people from all walks of life. Food is a way of bringing people of all communities together and a way of celebrating differences, through deliciousness.

One of the perks of being an Opera singer in America is the travel. Apart from frequently living out of a suitcase and being away from home, you get to eat at the local spots and try cuisines from all over the place. The food scene in the USA is an even bigger melting pot. Living in New York for two years, I was able to try the incredible Mexican and Cuban food that enrich Harlem all the way up into the Bronx, as well as countless "best in New York" pizza slices. But my favourite food in the USA is Cajun food. My experience of Cajun food is from South Louisiana. The unique flavour is a result of the huge French-Canadian influence combining with the early Spanish roots. You are left with food that has moments of Spanish, African and French, and when you mix that all together, you get Cajun cuisine.

Gumbo is one of the staples in South Louisiana and my roommate in New York shared his Grandmother's recipe with me. If I'm having a group of people over for dinner, this is what I tend to make. It's always a crowd pleaser and is unusual for my friends in Minnesota, where I am living now. The dish begins with making a dark roux, and the meat is usually a combination of shrimp, chicken and Andouille sausage—however this recipe just calls for chicken and sausage. Good luck and enjoy!!

Brown chicken in ½ cup of oil about 5 - 8min each side. Let chicken cool, debone chicken, place bones and skin in stew pot with water and boil for stock.

Make a roux. Add 3 cooking spoons of flour and vegetable oil. Cook on low heat stirring constantly until it turns the colour of caramel. Then, add vegetables and spices and cook until onion is translucent. Add chicken meat, chopped sausage and 7 cups of stock. Bring to boil, then simmer 45 minutes.

Add Filé powder as a garnish and thickener. Serve over rice.

1 - 2 lb whole chicken
8 cups of water
3 kitchen spoonful's of flour
3 kitchen spoonful's vegetable oil
2 cloves garlic, minced
1 onion, chopped
1 bell pepper, chopped
¾ cup celery, chopped
4 tbsp of Cajun spice of your choosing
1 lb andouille sausage
salt and pepper to taste
Filé powder (might have to get it online in NZ)

Sulphur Bay, Lake Rotorua

Winter sports on a Saturday morning; rugby, soccer, netball and hockey.

A day that is often cold and wet. There is always lots of cheering and encouragement from the sidelines, and of course the compulsory sausage sizzle!

"There is no substitute for hard work and application if you want to succeed".

All Black Captain Sam Cane

Beef Schnitzel

Sam Cane
Captain of the All Blacks rugby team and captain of the Chiefs in Super Rugby

My recipe isn't anything fancy but I love it! Growing up on the farm in Reporoa it was a favourite meal of mine—and still is. After travelling overseas for rugby for a few weeks, it is usually the first meal I cook after arriving home.

beef schnitzel
salt and white pepper
flour
egg
breadcrumbs
oil for frying

Season the meat with salt and white pepper. Coat lightly with flour, shaking off any excess, dip in egg and then coat with breadcrumbs, pressing the crumbs on firmly. Shallow fry in oil until golden brown on both sides.

Best served with kūmara chips, a fresh green salad and plenty of tomato sauce.

Signs on State Highway 5 at Reporoa and Mamaku

Tītī with Watercress and Kūmara

Wayne (Buck) Shelford, MBE
Former All Black Captain, Rugby Legend

Buck grew up in Rotorua and attended Western Heights High School. He became a much-revered captain of the All Black Rugby team in the 1980's and is credited with the revival of the All Blacks performance of the 'Ka Mate' haka.

Kai reka!
I love tītī as a kai, it's different and a real delicacy. Our Dad used to just boil it for hours in a traditional way. This recipe has an upmarket slant. Growing up in Rotorua was great with plenty to do for us kids, hanging out with our mates, riding our bikes everywhere, eeling, getting koura and fishing for trout. Good clean fun. I would like to acknowledge Ann Thorpe from her Kai Ora television series and her book for this wonderful recipe.

Bring large pot of water to the boil containing tītī. Simmer for 2 hours, (it smells really strong so leave windows open in kitchen). Turn off the heat, take out tītī and then pour off some of the stock. Replace with hot water to same amount and put in kūmara and watercress. Simmer until cooked.

Meanwhile preheat the grill until hot, place tītī in a roasting dish under grill for about 10 minutes until skin crisps up.

Place watercress on a plate and kūmara on the side. Break tītī up and place on watercress. Season and serve.

2 tītī (mutton birds)
large pot of watercress
6 small kūmara
salt and pepper

Lake Rerewhakaaitu

Beef Stir-fry with Black Bean Sauce

Sarah Walker
BMX Racer and former World Champion

Sarah is an elite BMX cyclist was New Zealand's first Olympic BMX medallist, winning Silver at the London Olympics in 2012 and 2009 Dual Elite Women BMX World Champ. She continues to race and is still often seen on the podium with her huge winning smile.

500g lean beef schnitzel
2 tbsp dark soy sauce
pepper
1 onion
2 stalks celery
3 tsp garlic
150g mushrooms
100g snow peas or green beans
1 – 2 tbsp black bean and garlic sauce

Cut the beef across the grain into thin strips. Mix with 1 tbsp dark soy sauce and a seasoning of pepper. Cover and set aside for 5 – 10 minutes. Heat a dash of oil in a large wok or frying pan. Over a high heat stir-fry the beef in two or three batches, until just browned. Do not overcook, remove the beef and set to one side. Reduce the heat; stir-fry the sliced onion for a few minutes and then add the finely sliced celery, minced garlic, sliced mushrooms and snow peas. Add the beef with the remaining soy sauce. Add the black bean and garlic sauce.

Toss together in the pan until very hot.

Ox Cheeks with Balsamic Glaze

This is a real winter-warming comfort food. The flavoursome meat is quite glutinous and ideal for long, slow cooking.

4 beef cheeks, trimmed
salt
pepper
2 tbsp vegetable oil
2 onions, diced
2 tbsp tomato paste
3 tbsp Dijon mustard
¼ cup balsamic vinegar
1 cup red wine
2 cups water
2 bay leaves

Preheat oven to 100º C. Heat the oil in an oven-proof dish; season the cheeks with salt and pepper and brown. Remove the meat and set aside. Add the onion and sauté until golden, add the tomato paste and mustard and sauté another 3 – 4 minutes, deglaze with vinegar. Add the wine and bay leaves and water.

Return the ox cheeks to the casserole and cover. Place in the oven and cook for 4 hours or until the cheeks are tender. Thicken the sauce with a little cornflour and water if desired.

Serve on a bed of creamed polenta and garnish with fried onion rings and parsley.

Beef and Beer Casserole

Helen Kessels

A winter warmer my husband, son and I particularly enjoy. My daughter not so much as it has parsnips!!! Easy to make and lovely with creamy mashed potato. The spices used are not to give it a Middle Eastern taste; they are added to give a bit more flavour and richness. You could use more or less as you prefer, or add your own favourites. I like the flavour that the celery and parsnips give to this dish; again this could be substituted with your own combination of favourite vegetables. Adding onion would also work but I am not a fan.

Cut the meat into chunks. Place the flour in a bowl and season with salt and pepper. Add the spices and mix together. Toss the meat through the seasoned and spiced flour. Heat the oil in a pan. Brown the meat, in batches if needed. Transfer meat to a casserole dish.

Quickly add the celery, parsnip, beef stock and tomato paste to the hot pan, stirring to mix and pick up any residue left from the seasoned meat. Pour the beer into the pan and simmer for 5 minutes. Transfer vegetables to the casserole dish and mix with the meat.

Place in a pre-heated oven at 180° C for 1¼ hours. If you have the time you can cook slower at 160° C for 1¾ hours.

Stir twice during the cooking and 15 - 20 minutes, prior to the finish stir through a couple of handfuls of fresh spinach leaves.

Serve with mashed potato and your favourite vegetables.

650 - 750g chuck or blade steak
¼ cup flour
salt and pepper
1 tsp coriander
1 tsp turmeric
½ tsp cumin
½ tsp nutmeg
2 tbsp oil
2 stalks celery, finely chopped
1 large parsnip
(peeled and finely chopped)
2 Continental Beef Stock Pots
(or Powdered Beef Stock)
1 - 2 tbsp tomato paste
330 ml bottle of beer
spinach

Bull's Eye

Ekaterina Bludova

My family and I came to Rotorua from St Petersburg in Russia in 2019. We like it here, the people are friendly and the sky is clean and blue. This recipe was handed down from my grandmother to my mother and then to me. No Russian family celebration is complete without this dish. This is a great hearty snack. Do not worry if the first time you do not get a perfect egg wrap, a little practice and everything will turn out!

Boil 4 eggs and peel them. Mix minced meat, onion and 1 raw egg, salt and pepper to taste. Minced meat should not be liquid. Wrap each egg in a ¼ of meat mixture.

Heat a frying pan with vegetable oil. Fry the eggs wrapped in minced meat on all sides until fully cooked.

Halve the cooked wrapped eggs, sprinkle with herbs (chives, parsley).

5 eggs
200 - 300g beef, minced
200 - 300g pork, minced
1 onion, grated
salt and pepper to taste
vegetable oil for frying
chives and parsley for garnish

Bitterballen

Carla Porter

This is a well-known appetiser in Holland; the bitterballs are usually served with a glass of ice cold 'Geneva' or Dutch gin. The original recipe uses veal, however as veal is not easily available in New Zealand, I use beef.

3 tbsp butter
5 tbsp flour
1 cup chicken stock
250g cold, cooked beef, shredded
1 tbsp parsley
salt and pepper
1 tsp Worcestershire sauce
oil for deep frying
2 egg whites
½ cup fine breadcrumbs
Dijon mustard

Heat the butter in a saucepan; add flour and cook—stirring slowly for 2 minutes. Gradually add the stock, stirring constantly until a thick paste is formed. Add the shredded cooked beef, parsley, salt, pepper and Worcestershire sauce, combine thoroughly. Spread the mixture onto a plate and refrigerate for two hours. Form the mixture into 1 inch balls. Dip the balls in the beaten egg white, and then roll in the bread crumbs. Deep fry a few balls at a time for 2 minutes or until golden. Drain on paper towels.

Serve piping hot with mustard on the side for dipping.

Nońa's Sweet and Sour Meatballs

Melanie Short

We all love this dish and when mum (Nońa) comes to stay she always brings it with her. Yummo.

Meatballs
500g beef mince
one sausage meat pack
one egg
¼ cup plum sauce
one packet mushroom soup

Mix together and roll into balls. Flour lightly and fry to light brown. Place in oven proof dish.

Sauce
1 cup of sugar
1 cup vinegar
4 tbsp tomato or plum sauce
4 tbsp soy sauce
6 tbsp Sherry

Bring to boil. Thicken with 4 teaspoons of cornflour and water.

Pour over meatballs and bake for half an hour.

Serve with rice and salad.

Slow Braised Oxtail Stew

Milani Thompson

My family and I are originally from South Africa, we immigrated here 13 years ago, and absolutely love living in Rotorua. There is everything we need within a short distance; Rotorua is surrounded by beautiful lakes, the ocean is 45 minutes away, and most importantly the people—everyone cares for one another in this town.

These two recipes, Slow Braised Oxtail Stew and South African Lamb Curry remind me of my childhood in South Africa, such comfort food. Both recipes include a fruit chutney and Mrs Ball's Fruit Chutney is a favourite from South Africa. I remember mum making these dishes in the pressure cooker, as she was pressed for time to get dinner on the table. I would always stand and watch her cook. I learnt to cook at a noticeably young age just from observing what mum was doing. I prefer to make these dishes when I have sufficient time, so that they can cook slowly in the oven.

1 medium onion, finely diced
1½ tsp garlic, chopped
1 kg oxtail, washed and well rinsed
45 ml red wine preferably, or white (optional)
1 tin crushed/chopped tomatoes
2 carrots, peeled and sliced
1 stick celery, thinly sliced
1 tsp beef stock powder or 1 beef stock cube
2 potatoes peeled and diced
or 500g baby potato's cut in half
⅓ cup peas (optional)
2 tbsp fruit chutney
1 tbsp Worcestershire sauce
1 tbsp tomato sauce

Pre-heat oven to 140° C. In an oven-proof casserole dish, fry the onions and garlic until golden, add garlic. Add the oxtail and brown on either side, add the wine and allow to reduce. Add the chopped tomatoes, sliced carrots, celery and beef stock powder, cover the oxtail with cold water. Place a sheet of baking paper over the meat, this will help keep the meat moist at all time and will prevent exposed meat from drying out.

Place in the oven and cook for 4 - 5 hours, until the meat is tender and nearly falling off the bones. Add the potatoes. Add a little more water if there is not enough liquid—does not need to cover the meat but needs to be sufficient that the casserole won't dry out. After 30 minutes remove from the oven. Add the peas, chutney, Worcestershire sauce and tomato sauce.

Traditional South African Lamb Curry

Milani Thompson

1 medium onion, finely diced
1½ tsp garlic, chopped
1½ tsp ginger, chopped
3 tsp mild curry powder
1 tsp garam masala
1 kg lamb shanks sliced into pieces or lamb shoulder chops
45 ml wine, preferably red or white (optional)
1 tin crushed/chopped tomatoes
salt to taste
2 carrots, peeled and sliced
2 potatoes, peeled and sliced
⅓ cup peas (optional)
3 tbsp fruit chutney

Pre-heat oven to 150° C. In an oven-proof casserole dish, fry the onions until golden, and then add garlic, ginger, curry powder and garam masala. Add the lamb and brown on either side, add wine and allow to reduce. Add the chopped tomatoes, salt and half a cup of water.

Place curry in the oven and cook for 1½ hours. Remove curry from oven and add carrots and potatoes. Add a little more water if there is not enough liquid. After 30 minutes remove from the oven. Add the peas and the chutney.

Serve with basmati rice and a tomato and onion salsa.

Lamb Tagine

A tagine is named after the earthenware pot that it is cooked in, you can also slow cook in the oven or in a large pot on your stove top. Use ready-to-eat fruit in a pouch, rather than dried fruit.

Heat the oil in the tagine or casserole dish. Season the meat with salt and pepper and brown on all sides, do this in batches. Set the meat aside. Add onions and garlic and sauté until golden. Add spices and sauté a further 2 – 3 minutes, then add the tomatoes.

Add the meat, cover and return to heat. Simmer slowly for 1 - 1½ hours until the meat is tender. Add the figs, prunes, olives and preserved lemon rind. Simmer for a further 4 – 5 minutes until heated through, add a little water if required.

Serve sprinkled with toasted almonds.

1 kg lamb shoulder, boned and cubed
olive oil
salt and pepper
5 onions, thinly sliced
2 cloves garlic, chopped
2 tbsp sweet paprika
1 tbsp ground cumin
1 tsp chilli powder
1 cinnamon stick
2 bay leaves
2 cloves
2 pinches saffron (optional)
400g can chopped tomatoes in juice
1 cup figs, halved
1 cup prunes
1 cup pitted green olives
2 preserved lemon rinds, washed and chopped
toasted almonds

Ohau Channel connects Lakes Rotorua and Rotoiti

Lamb with Prunes and Honey

Coral Day

This is an Iranian style dish originally from one of my favourite cookbooks, *Saraban* by Greg and Malouf. I initially cooked it when family were visiting and my eldest grandson enjoyed it so much, it became his flats signature dish for special occasions. It is a dish I enjoy and make often when having guests for dinner.

3 tbsp olive oil
1.2 kg lamb forequarter chops, cut into medium pieces
2 onions, cut into quarters
2 cloves garlic, roughly chopped
1 tsp ground ginger
1 tsp ground cinnamon
1 tsp sweet paprika
1 tsp sea salt
1 tsp freshly ground black pepper
1 litre good quality chicken stock
1 cinnamon stick
1 long strip orange peel, all pith removed
2 bay leaves
2 tbsp saffron liquid (optional)
3 tbsp honey
300g pitted prunes
saffron chelow rice and thick natural yogurt to serve

Heat 2 tbsp of the oil in a large, heavy-based frying pan. Brown the lamb in batches over a medium heat, then transfer to a large, heavy-based saucepan or casserole.

Pulse the onion and garlic to a coarse paste in a food processor. Add the remaining oil to the frying pan and fry the onion/garlic paste over a medium heat for 3 - 4 minutes, or until soft and translucent. Stir in the spices, salt and pepper and cook for a further 2 minutes, then add to the casserole. Pour in the chicken stock and stir well, then add the cinnamon stick, orange peel, bay leaves, honey and saffron liquid if you have it. Stir again and bring to the boil. Lower the heat and simmer, uncovered, for 1¼ hours, topping up with a little water if the mixture becomes too dry.

Add the prunes and cook for a further 35 - 40 minutes, squishing them into the sauce as they soften. At the end of the cooking time, the sauce should be thick and rich and the meat falling away from the bones. When ready to serve, taste and adjust the seasoning to your liking.

Serve with plain or chelow rice and plenty of creamy yogurt.

Sweet and Sour Sausages

Tricia Vickers

A winter warmer that always gets compliments!

500g sausages
2 tbsp oil
2 onions
1 cooking apple
½ cup sultanas
1 cup water
salt and pepper to taste
½ tsp ground ginger
1 dtspn soy sauce
1 tsp cornflour
1 tbsp cold water

Cook sausages by baking or frying and put to one side. Slice onions and sauté in hot oil. Dice peeled apple and sauté in pan. Stir in sultanas and first measure of water. Season with salt, pepper, ginger and soy sauce. Cover and simmer 3 minutes and then add the sausages cut in thirds and reheat.

Blend cornflour in second measure of water and stir in. Bring to boil and boil for 2- 3 minutes.

Serve with rice or other vegetables.

Lamb, Lemon, Spinach and Barley Stew

Mary Mathis

A tweaked version of an Irish stew. This is a popular meal when my family come home. I can cook it the day before and just add spinach, parsley and mint before serving. The cup of barley is enough to create a thick, creamy risotto-like stew.

Brown the lamb in batches and set aside. Reduce heat and sauté garlic, lemon peel, bay leaf, onion and carrot. Combine with the lamb and place in casserole dish. Add wine, barley and stock and mix well. Cook in moderate oven until the meat is tender. Just before serving add the spinach, mix well so it wilts and then add lemon juice, salt and pepper to taste. Lastly stir through the chopped parsley and mint.

Serve in shallow bowls and enjoy with a glass of pinot.

3 tbsp olive oil
1 – 1.5 kg lamb shoulder, bones and diced into 4cm pieces
peel of ½ lemon, finely diced
3 cloves garlic, finely chopped
1 fresh bay leaf
1 onion, finely diced
2 carrots, finely diced
100 ml dry white wine
1 cup pearl barley, well rinsed and drained
1 litre chicken stock
250 ml water (only add if too thick)
3 handfuls baby spinach leaves
juice of 1 - 2 lemons
3 tbsp chopped parsley and mint
salt and freshly ground pepper

Venison Sausage and Lentil Ragout

Sharon Ross

A family winter favourite, originally taken from Joan Bishop's *NZ Crockpot & Slow Cooker Cookbook* 2011.

Leave sausages whole or twist, and then cut in half at twist to form shorter sausages. Place in slow cooker. Add lentils, onion, lemon, garlic, ginger, tomato paste, chilli, kūmara, chicken stock and rosemary to slow cooker and stir.

Cover with lid and cook (crockpot—on high for 5 - 6 hours, slow cooker—high for 4½ hours). Taste and season with salt and pepper.

Serve garnished with fresh rosemary and lemon slices.

7 - 8 venison sausages (500-600g)
1 cup brown lentils, washed and drained
1 onion, finely chopped
1 lemon, cut into eights
3 cloves garlic, crushed
1½ tbsp minced ginger
3 tbsp tomato paste
½ - 1 tsp deseeded chilli, chopped
500g golden kūmara, peeled and diced into 2cm cubes
3½ cups chicken stock
2 tbsp chopped fresh rosemary
salt and pepper
sprigs of fresh rosemary and lemon slices to garnish

Matariki

Matariki (mata ariki - eyes of god or mata riki - little eyes), is the Māori name for the star constellation Pleiades that rises in the sky in mid-winter—signalling a change in the season with the arrival of the winter solstice, and beginning of the countdown to spring and summer. Matariki is celebrated as the start of the Māori New Year. A time to celebrate and gather with friends and family, a time for reflection of the past and being thankful to the gods of the land, forest and sea, and for the provisions of the past harvest—a time also for planning for the future. Sharing of food is important, and traditionally would often include a hāngi, where the food is cooked in an earth pit. A hole is dug and hot stones are placed in the bottom, baskets of meat and vegetables are then layered on top. The food is then covered with wet cloth and dirt, trapping the heat from the stones. The cooking process takes 3 – 4 hours. A good hāngi results in a succulent feast with a smoky flavour.

Matariki Slow-Roast Lamb

This is a slight twist on the traditional roast lamb. Smoking the lamb in the oven while roasting is inspired by the hāngi method of cooking. The recipe uses lamb, but we prefer hogget as it has more flavour.

1 leg of lamb

Dry Rub – mix together
3 tsp salt
2 tsp smoked paprika
1 tsp ground coriander
½ tsp freshly ground pepper

Rosemary Gremolata – mix together
4 cloves garlic, finely chopped
1 spray-free lemon zest
2 tsp fresh rosemary, chopped
¼ cup olive oil

For Smoking
1 – 2 cups manuka wood chips
2 twigs fresh rosemary
1 tsp raw sugar

For Gravy
250 ml chicken stock

Ask the butcher to remove the age bone and tie the lamb up with butcher's string. Rub the dry rub mixture well into the meat and then place on a baking rack.

Pre-heat oven to 120º C. Place the wood chips in a small tinfoil container and light them using a cooking gas torch, when burning/smoking well, add the sugar and twigs of rosemary. In a large roasting pan, place the tinfoil container of smoking woodchips in one corner. Pour 4 – 5 cups of water into the bottom of the roasting pan, be careful not to tip any water into the tinfoil, and then place the baking rack with prepared lamb on top. Massage the gremolata into the meat and cover the meat and roasting pan tightly with tinfoil, trapping the smoke inside.

Carefully place the roasting pan in the oven and cook for 3 - 3½ hours or until the meat is tender.

Remove from oven, discard the tinfoil and carefully remove the wood chip container. Increase oven temperature to 220º C. Using another roasting pan, return the uncovered leg of lamb still on the baking rack, to the oven to brown. Once browned remove from the oven and allow to rest for 5 – 10 minutes before serving.

While the lamb is browning make the gravy using the meat juices from the first roasting pan. Place roasting pan on a medium heat and add the chicken stock. Using a wooden spoon, scrape all the caramelised juices from the bottom of the pan. Thicken with a little cornflour dissolved in water and adjust seasoning. Remove any excess fat and strain.

Serve with roasted kūmara, pumpkin, potatoes and a green vegetable.

Overleaf: Lake Tarawera

Semolina Gnocchi with Grape Jelly

Chris Prenner

For the gnocchi
½ litre milk
250g semolina
1 - 2 eggs
salt
cinnamon stick
cloves
clarified butter

Bring the milk with some salt, cinnamon and cloves to the boil.

Remove the cinnamon and cloves and stir in semolina—let it cool for about 20 minutes, fold in the eggs.

Now form the gnocchi with two spoons. Alternatively, you can also roll it in to large noodles, breakfast sausage size.

Fry in clarified butter, roll in cinnamon sugar and serve with the grape jelly.

For the Grape Jelly

You can use white or red grapes, boil them up briefly with a very small amount of water. After 5 minutes push mixture through a muslin cloth. Measure the liquid, for every cup of liquid gained add ¾ cup of sugar slowly and bring to a boil. then simmer until setting point is reached. Test it occasionally by dropping a few drops of liquid onto a cold plate, place in freezer for a minute and test.

Enjoy it with some mulled wine. Hope you have some merlot left from the venison—see recipe on page 139—otherwise open another bottle.

Classic Citron Tart

Pastry
100g salted butter
200g high grade flour
60g castor sugar
1 egg
1 tsp vanilla

Grate the chilled butter coarsely, add the rest of the ingredients and knead into a pastry. You need to be quick so that the pastry doesn't get too warm.

Wrap in plastic and refrigerate for 30 minutes.

Roll out the pastry to 3.5mm - 4mm thick and lined a greased, floured 30cm flan tin, one with a removable bottom is best. Blind bake at 180° C until the pastry is very slightly coloured, approximately 10 minutes.

Remove from the oven and reduce the temperature to 130° C.

Filling:
200 ml cream
120 ml fresh lemon juice
6 eggs
250g castor sugar

Lightly whisk together the filling ingredients and then strain through a sieve. Fill the pastry shell with the citron mix and bake for 40 minutes.

Right: Thermal waterfall, Wai-O-Tapu

Spicy Apple Cake

In the 1970's *The New Zealand Radio and Television Cookbook*, edited by Alison Holst, was a national bestseller with nearly 400 pages of favourite kiwi recipes. D.E. Grayling from Katikati contributed this recipe and it has long been a go-to recipe for me when there are plenty of apples around. Very quick and easy to make.

Put apples in a mixing bowl and sprinkle with sugar, stir to coat and leave to stand for 2 – 3 minutes. Blend butter and egg into the apple. In a separate bowl sift together the dry ingredients.

Add the dry ingredients to the apple mixture and then lastly fold through the raisins and nuts. Pour into a greased cake tin, the mixture will be quite moist.

Bake at 180º C for 50 – 60 minutes. Cool for 10 minutes before turning out of the tin. Allow to cool completely before sprinkling with icing sugar.

1 cup apples, peeled, cored and chopped
1 cup sugar
125g butter, melted
1 egg, beaten
1½ cups flour
1 tsp baking soda
½ tsp salt
1 tsp cinnamon
½ tsp nutmeg
½ tsp allspice
½ cup sticky raisins
½ cup chopped walnuts

Apple and Date Cake

Gwen Ross

Great as a cake for afternoon tea or as a dessert, served with whipped cream.

Place apples, dates and baking soda in a bowl, pour over the boiling water and allow to cool. Beat together the butter and sugar until creamy, blend in egg and vanilla. Fold in flour and apple/date mixture.

Spread into a greased and lined 23cm spring form tin. Bake in oven at 180° C for 45 minutes. Remove to add topping.

Combine topping mixture in a saucepan and heat, stirring until butter is melted and sugar dissolved. Spread evenly over the cake. Return the cake to the oven and bake a further 15 minutes. Cool in the tin.

Cake Base
2 green apples, peeled and cubed
1 cup dates, chopped
1 tsp baking soda
1 cup boiling water
125g butter
1 cup brown sugar
1 egg
1 tsp vanilla essence
1½ cups flour, sifted

Topping
60g butter
2 tbsp milk
½ cup brown sugar
½ cup slivered almonds

Gwen's Fudge Cake

Judy Keaney
Former Mayoress

This recipe was given to me by Gwen a neighbour and was a firm favourite with my family. It featured very regularly in their school lunches as well as boarding school tuck boxes. I still make it for afternoon tea when I am hosting Mah Jong.

175g butter
100g sugar
2 dsp golden syrup
2 cups flour
2 tsp baking powder
sultanas and chopped walnuts as desired

Cream butter and sugar and add golden syrup followed by dry ingredients, sultanas and walnuts. Press into greased sponge roll tin and bake 30 mins at 180° C.

Fudge Icing
80g butter
3 tbsp milk
1 cup sugar

Boil together 3 mins and stir occasionally while boiling. Remove from heat and beat till thick. Pour the icing over the cake base and allow to set.

Lake Ōkareka walkway

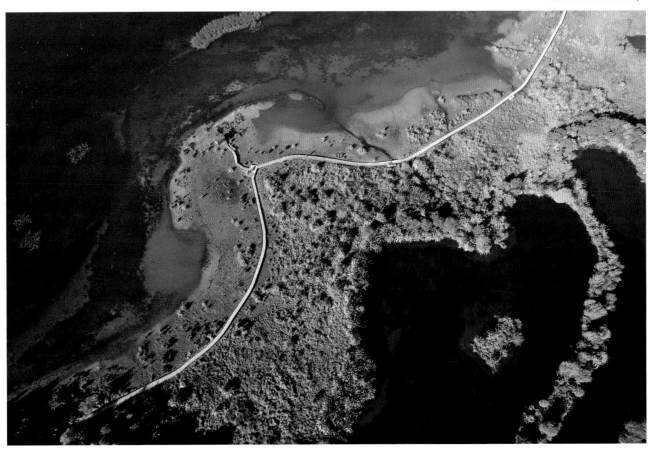

Walnut Fudge Recipe

Louw van Wyk's

We arrived in Rotorua in July 1978 and were the first South African family to live here. This recipe is based on Alison Holst's Fabulous Fudge recipe.

Mix all the ingredients except the walnuts and vanilla in the largest heat proof mixing bowl that will fit into your microwave oven. Microwave at full power for 9 minutes, stirring after 2, 4, 6 and 7 minutes.

When stirring, scrape all the sugar crystals from the sides of the bowl into the mix to ensure that they do not seed large sugar crystals in the fudge.

Test the fudge by pouring a small amount onto a cold plate. It should form small castles which stay upright. If not ready, microwave a further 2 minutes.

Add the vanilla and walnuts and beat for about 5 minutes with a wooden spoon until the mixture begins to keep its shape and does not flow off the spoon.

Pour into a square metal baking pan, 20 by 20 cm, which has been sprayed with cooking spray and then lined with non-stick silicon baking paper.

Allow to cool for an hour and then cut into small squares. Put squares onto a cooling rack to become a little firmer before packing into an airtight container.

If the fudge does not set, it has not been boiled for long enough. Put back into the heat proof mixing bowl and boil for two minutes more.

100g butter
1 cup sugar
¼ cup golden syrup
400g sweetened condensed milk
500 ml walnuts,
a mixture of halves and pieces
1 tsp vanilla

Famous English Fudge

Fay Olphert

I didn't name my fudge—other people have as it is quite tricky to make. The recipe came from an old English aunt many years ago. I have even bartered with my fudge—one acquaintance plucked and gutted wild duck for a batch of this fudge.

Bring all the ingredients to the boil in a thick bottomed large saucepan—do not allow it to boil until all sugar is dissolved, stirring consistently with a wooden spoon. It should reach soft ball stage in about 25 minutes. Test on a saucer. Remove from heat, add couple of drops of vanilla and beat well with wooden spoon until thick. Fold in the walnuts.

Pour into a greaseproof paper lined shallow baking tray and allow to set. Cut into squares and store in an airtight container.

½ lb granulated sugar
3 dsp golden syrup
6 oz butter
350 ml evaporated milk
couple drops vanilla
fresh walnuts, halved

Rotorua Mud Cake

A mud cake is a dense, moist, richly flavoured—almost fudgy, chocolate cake. Rotorua is well known for its boiling mud and there are several areas, including Kuirau Park in the centre of town, where visitors can watch the thick mud gurgle and bubble away. So, here is a recipe for Rotorua's mud cake, thick and gooey, and very chocolatey.

250g butter
250g dark chocolate, melted
(minimum of 70% cocoa solids)
100g castor sugar
80g brown sugar
400g hot water
20g coffee
185g self raising flour
23g cocoa powder
2 eggs
1 tbsp vanilla essence

In a large mixing bowl put the melted butter, melted chocolate, castor sugar, brown sugar, hot water, and coffee. Mix well until smooth. Sieve together flour and cocoa. Add to the chocolate mix, the eggs and vanilla, beat until combined. Fold in flour and cocoa.

Pour into a greased 23cm cake tin and bake at 150°C for approximately 50 minutes.

Below: Boiling mud, Wai-O-Tapu
Right: Champagne Pool, Wai-O-Tapu; Pohutu Geyser, Te Puia; Warbrick Terraces and Inferno Crater, Waimangu

Overleaf: Mt Ngāuruhoe

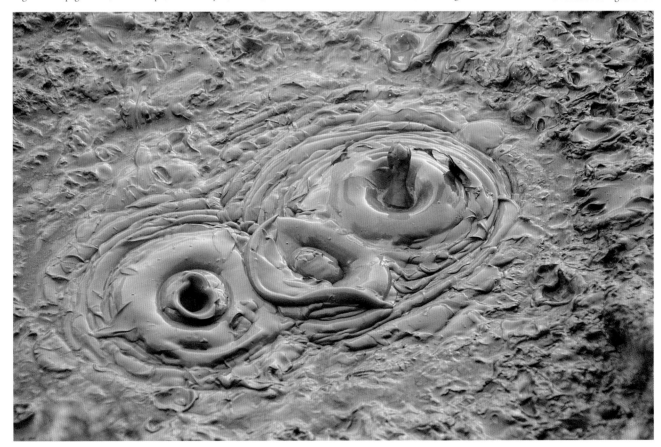

Recipe Index

About the Authors

Gerhard and Henrietta Egger have lived in Rotorua since 1993. Over the years, they have had a variety of careers, including (but not exclusively) hospitality and farming. Since 2003, Gerhard has been a professional photographer specialising in commercial and food photography and styling—and together they have published three previous books.

Volcanic Kitchens, come and join us, published in 2011. Gourmand World Cookbook Award winner, 'Best Photography Cookbook for New Zealand' and finalist in the 'Fundraiser Division for New Zealand, Australia and the Pacific'. Sales from *Volcanic Kitchens, come and join us* went towards supporting the Te Whakapono Health Trust and the Mahoro Dialysis Unit.

A Cut Above, cooking with AngusPure, published in 2014. A comprehensive book of beef recipes. Gourmand World Cookbook Award winner, 'World's Best Meat Cookbook'. Silver medal winner at the Independent Publisher Book Awards of America.

Source New Zealand, It's all about our food, our people, our land., published in 2017. Celebrating New Zealand's food producers, Gourmand World Cookbook Award winner, 'World's Best Photographer/Publisher'.

Acknowledgements

This book would not have come to fruition without the support of Jill Nicholas. A long time Rotorua resident and well-known journalist, Jill has worked extremely hard in the background contacting people, and, with a little bit of additional hassling, managed to cajole many of the recipes for us. Thank you for your never-ending enthusiasm, we could well have given up on this project if it were not for you and thank you also for writing the foreword.

Special thanks to Apumoana Marae, Owhata Marae, the lovely ladies from the Women's Health League, Tina Wirihina, Cate and Nabih Mansur, Achla and Shash Patel and their daughters, Zhongyue and daughter Cynthia Kouwenhoven and Chris Prenner. All of whom invited us into their homes or onto their Marae to photograph (and quality control). It was a privilege to be part of your lives in this small way, and we thank you all for the experience. Thanks to Paraone Pirika for writing the beautiful story of Hinemoa and Tūtānekai and to Ken Raureti for his story on Mount Tarawera.

Rotorua community—thank you to all who contributed recipes and stories—this book is about our community and could only have come together with your involvement.
Brita Marti, Joanne Bryant and Hilary Hape—all long-time friends. Thank you for your help and guidance in proof reading and your feedback on design and content.

To our daughter Luisa, because we love you exactly as you are.

Disclaimer

All photographs are Copyright © of Gerhard Egger Photography
Published in 2020 by Lasting Images, New Zealand
http://www.gerhardeggerphotographer.com
Photography: Gerhard Egger
Food styling and book design: Gerhard Egger
Text: Henrietta Egger

ISBN: 978-0-473-52883-6
A catalogue record for this book is available from the National Library of New Zealand

Prepress: **ICG** Creative. Content. Print
Printing: 1010 Printing